FORT MCKAVETT
AND TALES OF MENARD COUNTY

FORT MCKAVETT
AND TALES OF MENARD COUNTY

Clifford R. Caldwell

Copyright 2012
Clifford R. Caldwell

All rights reserved. No part of this book may be reproduced in any form, except for the inclusion of brief quotations for review, without the permission in writing from the author publisher.

All other interest and rights in the work, including but not limited to the right to grant or deny permission for further reproduction of the work, the right to use material from the work in subsequent works, and the right to redistribute the work by electronic means, are retained by the author.

ISBN 978-0-9842563-4-1

Printed in U.S. by Clifford R. Caldwell – 1 March 2012
First Edition

Contents

Introduction -	Menard County, Texas	1
Chapter I -	Mission Santa Cruz de San Sabá	7
Chapter II -	Fort McKavett	17
Chapter III -	John Monroe "Humpy" Jackson	62
Chapter IV -	John W. Vaden	78
Chapter V -	Silver & The Lost Bowie Mine	90
Chapter VI -	Menardville	98
Chapter VII -	Hext, Callan & Saline	116
Chapter VIII -	The Buffalo Soldiers	122
Chapter IX -	Stage Lines, Cattle Trails and Pegleg Station	138
Epilogue		150
Appendix		152
Bibliography		154
Index		164
About The Author		172

Foreword

Long before the shrill sound of the first bugler sounding reveille broke the still morning air at Fort McKavett Paleo-Indians had inhabited this region, dating to a time as early as 10,000 years ago. Spanish explorers followed in the sixteenth century, and found the Apache Indians had already resided in Central and West Texas, this being at the northern end of their range. Over time Comanches, Wichitas, Hasinais, Tonkawas, Yojuanes and Bidais began moving in, driving off the Apache. Eventually the Comanche prevailed, taking up residence and overpowering the other tribes...and many of the early Texas settlers.

Spanish missionaries, accompanied by a sizeable contingent of soldiers, reached the San Saba valley in 1753 and 1754 and established the first military garrison on the San Saba. It was almost a century before the 8th U.S. Infantry established an outpost on the San Saba in March 1852, choosing a location not far from the original Spanish post near Menardville. When Texas seceded from the Union at the onset of the Civil War the doors and windows of fledgling Fort McKavett were boarded up. The parade ground remained silent for years, apart of course from the brief occupation by the Confederate Army's Company E, 1st Texas Mounted Rifles. During the Civil War Indian depredations in the region spiked upwards, due in large part to the absence of the frontier fighting force. Finally, on 1 April 1868, Company A of the 4th United States Cavalry reopened Fort McKavett and took a hand in the defense of the local populace.

Sadly, after less than two decades of service, in August 1883 the remaining few troops at Fort McKavett were reassigned to Fort Clark near El Paso. The doors of Fort McKavett were shuttered for good. Another chapter in Texas' proud heritage had drawn to a close. Although a solid, historically accurate military history of Fort McKavett was undertaken a number of years ago, most earlier works lack much reference to the impact the black troopers had on the region, or the cowboys, outlaws, lawmen, cattle drives, Indian depredations or Spanish explorers that struggle to carve this Republic from the rugged countryside. Subjects of deeper historical interest such as these seem to have been passed over, thus the reader's opportunity to learn about these elements of local history has been greatly diminished.

The aim of *Fort McKavett, and Tales of Menard County* is to expand on the one dimensional look at the military history alone, and to explore the little known characters and fascinating tales that make up the fabric, and form the foundation, of the Fort McKavett and Menard County region...both good and bad.

Texans have always been a proud people. Our love of the Republic is frequently the butt of the joke on late night comedy television shows hosted by an array of overpaid, often coarse and morally vacant celebrities who seem to delight in portraying we common folk as buffoons. Studying, and writing about Texas history is an avocation followed by thousands. The material is virtually limitless, as are the interpretations. One does not need to be a historian to delight in our past. That makes each new book about Texas a discovery in itself.

At a celebration in his honor that took place on the evening of 5 January 1836, David Crockett, who had just arrived at Nacogdoches and would eventually meet his fate at the Alamo, shared a colorful and popular story about his departure from politics when he was most recently defeated in his attempt to win a seat in Congress, closing with the popular and immortal line "...you may all go to hell, and I will go to Texas."[1] If only one had a penny for each time those words have been uttered, or quoted, over the past 175 years! Granted, David Crockett spent only a couple of months in Texas but he had the highest of hopes for the soon to be founded republic.

---

[1] David Crockett. 1834.

To Texans, the names of heroes like Crockett, James Bowie, William Barret Travis and Juan Nepomuceno Seguin occupy a special place in our hearts. The mere mention of the epic saga at the Alamo can cause tears to well up in the eyes of otherwise rugged and fearless Texas men. The notion that, as one popular author recently penned, "Texans also use the Alamo and the revolt against Mexico to establish a republic and, later, a state that they believe unique and more special than any other..." is inherently offensive to all real Texans. First of all, Texas is "...unique and more special than any other [state]."[2] It is a fact that Texas pride runs strong, perhaps stronger than any other state. Who would want to live in a place where they proudly boast "...there is nothing special about our state?" Somehow the author's words sound like an apology for Texas exceptionalism. Most offensive, however, is the suggestion that Texans would use the fall of the Alamo as an excuse for having broken away from Mexico. Apparently the author only had enough time to conduct superficial research into the underlying conflict between Texas colonists and Mexico prior to penning those lines, laying off much of the contrariety to differing positions on slavery. The Alamo became a rallying cry perhaps, but not an excuse.

In an unfortunate choice of passage, the same author went on to cite Mexican General Antonio López de Santa Anna y Pérez de Lebrón who he claims "...was puzzled as to why this province of his republic still allowed slavery" and that Texans "believe that their independence was bought and paid for at the Alamo."[3] The only part this popular littérateur got right was that Texans do believe that our independence was "...bought and paid for at the Alamo."[4]

For the record, Santa Anna was an abysmally bad general who made one colossal blunder after another and tried to compensate for his military incompetence by his brutality...but to no avail. It is one of the puzzles of Mexican history that Santa Anna was able to gain political power in Mexico so many

---

[2] Wallis, Michael. 2011. *David Crockett, The Lion of the West.* W.W. Norton. New York, New York: p 289.

[3] Ibid. p 282.

[4] Ibid. p 282.

times despite his record of ineptitude. Those who believe that Santa Anna was a benevolent man, opposed to slavery, might wish to study the matter further, or consider the accounts of "The Yellow Rose of Texas," or the fact that hundreds of his soldiers perished on the brutal trek north to San Antonio de Béxar in the dead of winter in 1836.[5] This is the same Santa Anna that, at the battle of San Jacinto, was unable to rally his men against an inferior force of Texican's, stole an enlisted man's uniform and ran like a coward.

In any case, detractors feel free to besmirch Texans because we have broad shoulders and quietly endure the raillery. At the end of the day we know we are blessed with something special in the Lone Star State. I hope that readers will thoroughly enjoy learning more about Fort McKavett, Menard County, and some of the fascinating incidents that have taken place there. The Fort McKavett story is an important chapter in the proud history of the Lone Star State.

---

[5] The Yellow Rose of Texas, an attractive mulatto slave girl, is fancifully famous for bedazzling Santa Anna out of his trousers at the Battle of San Jacinto on 12 April 1836.

Acknowledgements

Properly acknowledging the many kind individuals who aided, and provided the inspiration for this book is a joy and not a chore. Recalling the many telephone calls, conversations, e-mails and written contributions generously offered by friends, fellow authors, historians and researchers reminds one that practically everyone involved in non-fiction history is an eager contributor, anxious to freely share their knowledge. Attempting to thank everyone is a daunting task, and one always feels as though someone has been left out.

Countless friends and fellow historians have generously offered their assistance, sending manuscripts, articles and photos. My dear friend Joseph Luther, perhaps the most knowledgeable person I know when it comes to local Indian and military history, took a hand when needed. Fellow authors and historians David Johnson, Bob Alexander, Chuck Parsons and Ron DeLord all contributed valuable material and urged me on to dig deeper into "Humpy" Jackson and John Vaden. The published works of Frederica Burt Wyatt, Jerry M. Sullivan, and The Friends of Fort McKavett State Historic Site provided valuable insight and sound historical material.

Special thanks go to John and Katherine Kniffen of the Menardville Museum and Menard Historical Society at Menard, Texas. Their knowledge and assistance as well as their kindness and generous gift of their time, aided greatly in the development of this text. I also wish to acknowledge Cody Mobley, Curator of the Fort McKavett State Historical Site, who also gave freely of his valuable time and provided a great deal of useful information about Fort McKavett.

Bryant Saner of the Hill Country Archaeology Society provided valuable information concerning the geology and early inhabitants of the Hill Country region. His assistance was truly invaluable.

Menard County seems to be full of friendly and helpful folks and tireless volunteers who are interested in history and willing to help all that inquire. Alicia Brown, local historian and volunteer for the TxGenWeb Project, helped immensely, graciously sharing her research and cross checking mine.

The archives of the Haley Memorial Library and History Center at Midland, Texas are filled with material from a variety of collections, including that of author and historian J. Evetts Haley who wrote *Fort Concho an the Texas Frontier*. Haley's file on "Humpy" Jackson proved to be a valuable resource. Many thanks to J. P. "Pat" McDaniel and the entire staff at the library for their assistance.

Although there is no substitute for primary sources and grass roots research, the bibliography section of this book is loaded with the names of authors whose earlier works contributed much to my exploration of Fort McKavett and Menard County. All deserve special recognition.

Introduction

Menard County, Texas

*A man travels the world over
in search of what he needs
and returns home to find it.*
George Moore

Menard County is located in Central Texas, although most locals seem to identify more readily with it being part of West Texas. Menard borders Concho, McCulloch, Mason, Kimble, Sutton, Schleicher, and Tom Green counties. The county seat is located in Menard, formerly called "Menardville." The name change occurred as a result of one of those little historical quirks that abound in Texas. Fort Worth and Rio Grande Railroad Company officials asked residents to drop the "ville" and rename their town Menard in order to facilitate the painting of signs. Menardville residents, anxious to have the railroad come to town, complied.

The San Saba River crosses the county from west to east, and is fed by numerous springs and small streams. The county consists of 902 square miles of largely hilly terrain on the Edwards Plateau at elevations ranging from 1,700 to 2,400 feet above sea level. Paleo-Indians inhabited this region as early as 10,000 years ago. When early Spanish explorers arrived in the sixteenth century they found the Apache Indians in Central and West Texas. The region near Menard County was at the northern end of the Apache's range. Over time the Comanches began moving down from the north in the eighteenth century, eventually supplanting the Apache over time. The Spanish began exploring the San Saba valley in 1753 and 1754. They had hoped to attract the Apache Indians to the mission, given the favorable terrain and well watered location. Unfortunately their plan turned out to be a colossal blunder. The Apache were more concerned about the raiding Comanches, Wichitas, Hasinais, Tonkawas, Yojuanes and Bidais who were eventually successful in their efforts to push them out of the area.[6] In the meantime, Comanche, Wichita and Caddo warriors sacked the mission on the San Saba River near Menardville in March 1758, quickly bringing the Spaniard's plans to a premature and deadly conclusion.

Menard County was formed by the state legislature in 1858 from Bexar County, and was named for Michel Branamour Menard, the founder of Galveston.[7] Menardville and Camp San

---

[6] John, Elizabeth A.H. 1981. *Storms Brewed in Other men's Worlds: The Confrontation of Indians, Spanish and French in the Southwest – 1540-1795*. College Station, Texas: Texas A&M University Press. pp 158-160

[7] Michel Branamour Menard was an Indian trader, entrepreneur, and founder of the Galveston City Company. Menard was the only son of Michel B. and Marguerite (de Noyer) Menard, born 5 December 1805, at La Prairie, near Montreal, Quebec Canada. Menard became a fur trader at Detroit in about 1820, and worked his way into the Minnesota area. While working for his uncle he became a resident trader to a band of Shawnees living near Ste. Genevieve, Missouri. Menard was chosen a chief, and moved with the tribe to the White River in Arkansas Territory. He later removed to the Red River below Pecan Point in 1828. On 1 December 1829 Menard applied for citizenship in Nacogdoches, where he continued to collect skins and furs from the Shawnees and other Indian tribes. By 1834 he owned 40,000 acres, scattered from the lower Trinity River above Liberty to Pecan Point. He built a combination sawmill and gristmill on Menard Creek in 1833, which he operated with the aid of his cousin and other relatives.

Menard represented Liberty County at the Convention of 1836. Although he personally believed independence impractical, he bowed to the majority will and signed the Texas Declaration of Independence. Among Menard's land speculations was the 1834 arrangement to acquire title to land on the eastern end of then vacant Galveston Island. The site was forbidden to non-Hispanic Texans without permission from the president of Mexico. Unable to develop it prior to 1836, his title was questioned by rival claimants during the First Congress of the Republic of Texas. He had to pay the republic $50,000 to clear his title and had to take in many other partners besides the original investors, Samuel May Williams and Thomas F. McKinney. The Galveston City Company was organized in April 1838 and began issuing deeds to investors and purchasers. Menard, as Texas commissioner, unsuccessfully sought a loan from the United States for the new republic in 1836-1837 and represented Galveston in the Fifth Congress, 1840-1841. He married four times. His first wife, Marie Diana LeClerc of St. Genevieve (1832) died of cholera aboard a ship en route to Texas from New Orleans on 14 May 1833. He married his second cousin, Adeline Catherine Maxwell

Saba attracted early settlers, but the withdrawal of troops from Camp San Saba in 1859, and the threat of Indians attacks, delayed new settlement and caused many established residents to leave. The handful of remaining dwellers attempted to organize the county government in 1866, but when their efforts failed the legislature placed Menard County under the jurisdiction of Mason County. When Fort McKavett was opened in 1868, people once again moved into the area. Menard County residents finally elected their own officials in 1871.

Menard County Courthouse circa 1885
Courtesy of the Menardville Museum

In 1870, Menard County had a population of 667, of whom 295 were white and 372 were black. The high percentage of black residents was a result of the presence of the "Buffalo Soldiers" at Fort McKavett.[8] By 1880 the county's population

---

(1837), but she died during the yellow fever epidemic in Galveston in July 1838. Next he wed Mary Jane Riddle (1843). She died in 1847. His fourth wife was Rebecca Mary Bass, a widow with two daughters whom Menard adopted in 1850, the same year the couple became parents of a son. Menard struggled to make his speculations and businesses more profitable.

Unfortunately no two accounts of his life are the same, due to his monstrous tales to friends and family. He died at home in Galveston on 2 September 1856, and is buried at the Catholic Cemetery in Galveston.[7]

[8] The used of the term "Buffalo Soldier" throughout the text is a generic reference to black cavalry and infantry soldiers who were, during the time

had risen to 1,239, but the number of black residents had fallen to only 37 as a result of the Buffalo Soldier's departure. When Fort McKavett was eventually closed for good in 1883 the population fell precipitously, but by 1890 it had almost recovered, boasting 1,215 residents. Fort McKavett had about eighty residents in the 1890s, Menardville 300. The balance was spread throughout the rural area. In terms of ethnicity, most of the immigrants who came to Menard County had come from England, Ireland, and Germany during the 1870s, and from Mexico during 1880s and again in the 1930s.[9]

Prior to the turn of the last century more than three-quarters of the county's population lived on farms and ranches. Stock raising was the dominant occupation, with 10,456 head of cattle and 27,586 sheep in 1880, to 33,690 cows and 90,363 woolies in 1890. The number of ranches grew from thirty-six in 1880 to 158 by 1890, and their average size increased from 1,811 to 2,096 acres.[10] Although most of the county's land was devoted to livestock raising, some irrigated pastures along the San Saba River provided crops such as cotton, corn, sorghum, oats, alfalfa, rye, and wheat.

With the aid of incentives offered by the county including a right-of-way, land for stock pens and depot, and $10,000 to build the station itself, the Fort Worth and Rio Grande Railroad Company extended its track to Menardville. In February 1911 the first train arrived. With the addition of rail service, citizens of the region could reach outside markets easier. The population of the town of Menardville boomed. By 1914 the population reached roughly 1,000.

For quite some time the cattle industry dominated sheep production in Menard County, with the number of cattle rising to more than 54,000 and the number of sheep falling to fewer than 19,500. However, by the 1920s the wool industry in the

---

period covered by this writing, posted at Fort McKavett and various other forts throughout Texas.
[9] Vivian Elizabeth Smyrl, "MENARD COUNTY," *Handbook of Texas*. Citing - Menard County Historical Society. 1982. *Menard County History-An Anthology*. San Angelo, Texas: Anchor. Also citing Menard *Messenger*. Historical Edition. And - 18 June 1936. Menard *News*. Historical Edition. 11 November 1971.
[10] Ibid.

region caused a shift, with the sheep population growing to more than 71,000 and cattle falling to less than 28,000 head. Wool production peaked in 1930, when 305,450 sheep produced more than 2.1 million pounds of wool.[11] In the latter years the county had more than 35,700 goats and produced nearly 111,600 pounds of mohair.

As was the case in most of rural Texas, the 18th amendment to the U.S. Constitution and the subsequent Volstead Act of 28 October 1919 prohibiting the manufacture and sale of alcohol was pretty much a non-event for Menard County residents. The population, largely of European ancestry, continued to manufacture and consume beer and whiskey as they had previously, but did so discretely.

During the Great Depression Menard County escaped much of the hardships experienced by the more urban areas of Texas. The depression shifted the focus of local agriculture away from cotton and back to feed crops. In 1940 only 1,470 acres were planted in cotton. Oats, barley, sorghum, and hay became the primary crops, which together accounted for more than sixty percent of the county's harvest.

Although wildcatters had been drilling exploratory wells since 1919, oil and gas production did not begin until the 1940s. The first attempted oil well, drilled in 1919, produced a dry hole. A gas deposit was tapped in 1929, but was plugged the same year for lack of a market until it was re-drilled in 1941, after which it produced about seven million cubic feet of gas. A small oilfield was discovered northeast of Fort McKavett in 1946, but was abandoned the following year. In spite of the fact that exploration continued throughout the 1940s and 1950s, it was not until the 1960s that any truly important deposits were found. Production peaked in that decade, with an average annual yield of more than 270,000 barrels. Of the county's forty oilfields, about twenty were still active in the 1980s, producing 132,000 to 185,000 barrels annually.[12]

At present, more than ninety percent of the land in Menard County is dedicated to farming, ranches, and wildlife related enterprises. Less than five percent is under cultivation. The

---

[11] Ibid.
[12] Ibid.

population continued to slip from its peak of 4,521 in 1940 to a present day estimate of 2,242.[13] The exodus does not trouble residents however. The county remains one of the more picturesque in the state, inhabited by a diverse group of friendly and resilient folks!

---

[13] US Census Bureau. *QuickFacts*. Revised Friday, 3 June 2011.

Chapter I

Mission Santa Cruz de San Sabá

Men will wrangle for religion, write for it, fight for it, die for it, anything but live for it.
Charles Caleb Colton

On Thursday 16 March 1758, the tranquility of an otherwise peaceful spring morning in the Texas Hill Country was shattered when an onslaught of Indians, many brandishing firearms, swept down on the tiny outpost called Mission Santa Cruz de San Sabá, near present day Menard. The church's compound, comprised of wooden palisades, was quickly surrounded by a force of about 2,000 hostile Wichita, Comanche, and Caddo warriors.[14,15,16] The three Spanish priests in residence tried to appease the Indian force with gifts of tobacco and offers of safe passage to the nearby Presidio, but

---

[14] One source indicates that the raiding Indian party was comprised largely of Apaches. See - Nathan, Paul D. translator. Forward by Weddle, Robert S.. 2000. *The San Sabá Papers*. Dallas, Texas: Southern Methodist University Press.

[15] John, Elizabeth A. H.. 1975. *Storms Brewed in Other Men's Worlds: The Confrontation of Indians, Spanish, and French in the Southwest, 1540–1795*. College Station, Texas: Texas A&M University Press.

[16] From the 1750s to 1810 one band of the Wichita Indians was on the Red River north of the site of present Nocona, Texas. The Wichitas, during this period, were prominent middlemen in the trade between the Comanches on the plains and Louisiana merchants and were at the pinnacle of their power and prominence. Warriors of the band accompanied the Comanches in the attack on Mission San Sabá Mission in 1758. Their Red River villages withstood a retaliatory strike by the Spanish in 1759.

the palisade was soon overwhelmed with the armed hostiles. Two of the three missionaries, including the president of the mission Father Fray Alonso Giraldo de Terreros and Father Fray Joseph de Santiesteban lost their lives. Santiesteban's severed head was found in the clothing storeroom after the assault.[17] The third priest, Father Fray Miguel de Molina, was shot in the right chest by a musket ball that was fired at him through the window of his private quarters by one of the raiding Indians. Amazingly, Father Molina managed to survive. The remainder of the mission's occupants took shelter in the sanctuary building, the compound's largest structure. Several structures, including the mission's palisade, were set ablaze.[18] Some inhabitants who had retreated to their enclosed rooms fired at the Indians through portholes that had been fashioned in the walls for such a purpose. Although their efforts were valiant, the opposing force was far too large for their retaliatory fire to dissuade. Along with the priests six soldiers were slain during the incident.

When the warlike force had first arrived at the mission it was under the pretense of a peaceful visit, but soon after their entrance they began firing their weapons and stealing horses. The Indians laid waste to the compound and began celebrating their victory. Sporadic fighting continued as the hostiles fired their muskets at the church sanctuary and tried to gain entry.[19,20]

---

[17] Nathan, Paul D. translator. Forward by Weddle, Robert S.. 2000. *The San Sabá Papers*. Dallas, Texas: Southern Methodist University Press. p 98.

[18] One source reported that "... a force of 2000 Comanches and their allies attacked the mission of Santa Cruz de San Sabá, burning it to the ground and killing thirty-five people, including the head friar. In a follow-up attack, the Comanches killed twenty soldiers and stole 700 head of livestock. The next year, the Spanish sent a punitive military expedition from Mexico, but their forces were badly defeated by the Wichitas." See – Texas State Library & Archives Commission. *Indian Relations in Texas*. 2 March 2011.

[19] Citing Handbook of Texas. John, Elizabeth A. H.. 1975. *Storms Brewed in Other Men's Worlds: The Confrontation of Indians, Spanish, and French in the Southwest, 1540–1795*. College Station, Texas: Texas A&M University Press.

[20] The 1728 musket, with modifications made in 1746, was the musket carried by the majority of French troops during the French and Indian War. Changes in the 1740s included the standardized use of a steel ramrod in 1743 and, after 1746, newly manufactured muskets had the frizzen pan bridle removed. There were three arsenals making the 1728/1746 .69 caliber models, including Charleville, Maubeuge, and St. Etienne. St. Etienne was

In a deposition taken some time after the incident Joseph Gutiérrez, who was a servant at the Mission San Sabá, claimed that the Indians were armed with French made firearms, large powder horns, pikes, bows and arrows, muskets and cutlasses. All of the warriors were festooned in typical Indian war costume.[21]

Entrance to Presidio San Luis de las Amarillas – Menard, Texas
Photo from Author's Collection

Sergeant Joseph Antonio Flores, who was garrisoned at the Presidio San Luis de las Amarillas and involved in the fight, provided a gripping account afterwards. At the request of Father Fray Alonso Giraldo de Terreros, Flores had led a patrol to a hill just beyond the nearest ford on the river south of the mission. From his elevated post he observed a large group of Indians on the trail leading towards the mission. Flores

---

the largest producer and because of this the 1728 is often called the St. Etienne musket.
[21] See - Nathan, Paul D. translator. Forward by Weddle, Robert S.. 2000. *The San Sabá Papers*. Dallas, Texas: Southern Methodist University Press. p 44.

attempted to retreat to the mission and warn those within, but he and his men quickly came under fire. Three of his men, Joachin García, Luis Thorino and Joseph Vásquez were killed almost instantly.[22]

Mission Santa Cruz de San Sabá Historical Marker – Menard, Texas
Photo from Author's Collection

---

[22] Ibid. pp 46-60.

Site of Mission Santa Cruz de San Sabá – Menard, Texas
Photo from Author's Collection

Breastworks at Presidio San Luis de las Amarillas – Menard, Texas
Photo from Author's Collection

Four miles upstream, the thirty soldiers at the Presidio San Sabá heard the terrible commotion and saw the smoke from the fires. Before long they themselves were surrounded. Their numbers that day were reduced by two-thirds of the garrison's force who were away on various excursions. Thus, while the soldiers were able to keep the Indians at bay, they could not come to the rescue of the mission.[23]

As night fell, the victorious Indians celebrated their victory a short distance from the beset missionaries. They feasted by roasting several slaughtered oxen they had stolen from the mission compound. While the Indians were distracted by their jubilant banquet, the survivors led by Juan Leal, escaped under cover of darkness and made their way to the Presidio. Many of them were badly wounded.

On 20 March 1758 Don Toribio de Urrutia, Commandant of the fort at San Antonio de Béjar, sent word of the disaster to his superiors, writing:

> *Your worship is hereby appraised of a letter, dated the sixteenth of the current month of March, from Colonel Don Diego Ortiz Parrilla, informing me that he is under attack by more than 2,000 Comanche Indians and other allied nations, all equipped with firearms. At the same time they attacked the mission that is in his charge. He believes it to have been demolished and all the religious and other inhabitants killed, for it was impossible for the aid Colonel to supply sufficient reinforcements.* Urrutia later added...*I regard that Presidio as already destroyed.*

---

[23] Citing Handbook of Texas. John, Elizabeth A. H.. 1975. *Storms Brewed in Other Men's Worlds: The Confrontation of Indians, Spanish, and French in the Southwest, 1540–1795*. College Station, Texas: Texas A&M University Press.

Private Quarters Inside Presidio San Luis de las Amarillas – Menard, Texas
Photo from Author's Collection

The following day the various groups of soldiers who had been on foray returned to the Presidio and provided needed reinforcements, apparently saving the garrison from the near total destruction the mission had experienced.

On 20 March 1758 Don Toribio de Urrutia requested that additional troops be sent to San Antonio, "…inasmuch as the Presidio of San Luis de las Amarillas on the San Sabá is under attack." Eventually some were sent, but not in time to have any impact on the outcome of this incident. Soon both the mission and the presidio would vanish from the landscape.

**Inside the Entrance to Presidio San Luis de las Amarillas
Menard, Texas**
Photo from Author's Collection

The site of Mission Santa Cruz de San Sabá is located on present day FM 2092, about three miles east of Menard. Colonel Diego Ortiz Parrilla led a march from San Antonio to this spot on the San Saba River on 5 April 1757. Most of the party, which consisted of a large force of soldiers, six missionaries, and assorted others totaling 300 in all, arrived at the site on 17 April 1757. Ortiz Parrilla spent five days exploring the riverbanks in search of a suitable locale. Once selected, he laid out the presidio on the north side of the San Saba River. Friars quarters were built from available native timber. Believing that the distance between the presidio and the mission would reduce the possibility of the soldiers harassing the Indians and a temporary church site was located downstream four and one half miles from the presidio on the south bank. Unfortunately the friars failed to consider the fact that the distance would make the mission more vulnerable to attack.

Work on the first of the two projected missions begun almost at once. In mid-June friars were encouraged when roughly 3,000

Apaches, traveling north to hunt buffalo and fight the Comanches, camped near the mission site. Unfortunately for the friars, the Indians were unresponsive to the missionaries' efforts to bring them to Christianity however.

Three of the missionaries decided that the project was doomed to failure and withdrew. Plans to begin a second mission were abandoned. Scarcely eleven months later Mission Santa Cruz de San Sabá, and soon after Presidio San Luis de las Amarillas, would fade into history. Burned and plundered the Mission Santa Cruz de San Sabá was not repatriated. Presidio San Sabá was strengthened. It managed to survive for another decade, in part due to its perceived role in the Spanish mining operations nearby. In time it too was abandoned when no substantial silver deposits were found.

The ruins of the Presidio San Luis de las Amarillas remained as visible reminders of the Spanish presence. But the remnants of the sacked mission, never substantial to begin with, continued to crumble until recently. Historians and archeologists began trying to relocate Mission San Sabá in the mid-1960s, but it was not until 1993 that the search met success.

In spite of the fact that the Spanish frontier had been pushed much further north than the Mission Santa Cruz de San Sabá, it now began to retreat southward at a steady pace. The Spaniards, followed by the Mexicans, began to lose their grip on control of Texas as more and more Anglo settlers arrived. In less than eight decades it too slipped away... forever.

Chapter II
Fort McKavett

The muffled drum's sad roll has beat The soldier's last tattoo; No more on Life's parade shall meet The brave and fallen few. On Fame's eternal camping-ground Their silent tents are spread, And Glory guards, with solemn round The bivouac of the dead.
Theodore O'Hara

Historians often feel compelled to begin each story as renowned author James Michener might - starting with the earliest date in history when intelligent life was formed, then slowly and deliberately working forward in time. This author has resisted that urge, although powerful, and selected a point of beginning somewhat more recent.

Background...

It is important to note that while *Fort McKavett, and Tales of Menard County* deals primarily with the period beginning with Texas independence from Mexico, the San Sabá River Valley region near Fort McKavett has supported human habitation for several thousand years. Archeological evidence indicates that hunter-gatherers established themselves in the area as early as 10,000 years ago. Early Spanish explorers found the Apache Indians in Central and West Texas in the 1500s, and the Comanches began moving down from the north in the 1700s. The Spanish explored the San Saba valley in 1753 and 1754. In April 1757, Father Alonso Giraldo de Terreros founded Santa Cruz de San Sabá Mission, hoping to Christianize the Apache Indians. San Luis de las Amarillas Presidio, under the command of Diego Ortiz Parrilla, was established nearby to provide protection for the mission. In 1761, Felip de Rábago y Terán replaced Ortiz Parrilla and improved the presidio by replacing wooden structures with stone ones.[24]

Even though an initial missionary trip in 1629 had been made, the first mission in Texas was established in 1632, near present-day San Angelo. The 1632 mission existed for six months before it was abandoned due to its remoteness from the home base at Santa Fe, New Mexico. This mission is believed to have been located near the confluence of the Concho and Colorado Rivers, and was known as Río San Clemente. In 1680, the Indians at Santa Fe, New Mexico revolted, causing the Spanish settlers there to flee and take refuge in the El Paso area. Along with the Spanish came friendly Indian tribes who settled along the Rio Grande. Here, the Franciscans began the missions of Corpus Christi de la Isleta (Ysleta), Nuestra Señora de la Limpia Concepción del Socorro and San Antonio de Senecú.[25]

In 1683-1684 Juan Domínguez de Mendoza and Father Francisco Lopez de Mendoza Grajales led an exploratory journey into Texas that reached as far northeast as the Fort McKavett area. The Mendoza-López Expedition set out 15 December 1683, heading southeast from El Paso along the Rio Grande to La Junta. From there, they headed north to the Pecos River, and followed it a short distance before crossing near present-day Horsehead Crossing. The expedition broke off from the river and took up a course east across a plain to the Middle Concho, which according to their journal they followed to its junction with the Nueces River near San Angelo. Mendoza next continued east to a river that he called the San Clemente, but in actuality was probably the Colorado, near its union with the Concho.

In one author's account, when Mendoza arrived at the junction of the Conchos he is not clear if he means the Middle and South Concho or the Main Concho and North Concho. There is a six-mile difference between theses. The same source, in his analysis of the Mendoza-López Expedition journals, moves the expedition south to the dry head of Lipan Creek,

---

[24] Menard County Historical Society. 1982. *Menard County History-An Anthology*. San Angelo, Texas: Anchor.
[25] "The Spanish Missions in Texas." by Robert Plocheck. Associate Editor. *Texas Almanac 2006–2007*.

then to the springs at the head of Kickapoo Creek. From that point Mendoza is said to have headed south to the San Saba River, between Fort McKavett and the old presidio and mission at present day Menard.[26]

The expedition party remained there for six weeks, then returned to El Paso in May 1684. Their diary describes the route of the expedition, the land, agriculture and rivers of the region. Following their journey, Father López and Mendoza went to Mexico City to urge the Spaniards to occupy the lands they traveled with missionaries and soldiers. Their recommendations were ignored.[27]

The first missionary efforts in the area of El Paso del Norte were on the Mexican side of the Rio Grande in the 1630s. After failed attempts, a temporary church was built in 1656 and a successful mission was founded in 1659. There were subsequent missions in the area, and some sources say the Senecú mission was established soon after 1659 and before the refugees arrived from New Mexico in 1680. In 1684, a second mission in the area of San Angelo existed from March to May. Its location was near the juncture of the Colorado River and the Concho River. Others, however, place this mission farther east, on the South Llano River and the San Saba River.[28] More recent research of historic Spanish documents accompanied by physical and archaeological discovery point to the possibility that additional missions, mentioned in early Spanish text, were established along the San Saba River, further east of Menard as well as in southern Kerr County.[29]

---

[26] Hays, Jet. A New Technique for Delineating Aboriginal Trade and Spanish Colonial Expedition Routes and the Route of the Mendoza-Lopez Expedition. MA Thesis. Texas Tech University. May 1998. pp 17-39.
[27] Imhoff, Brian. 2002. *The Diary of Juan Domínguez de Mendoza's Expedition into Texas (1683-1684): A Critical Edition of the Spanish Text with Facsimile Reproductions.* Dallas, Texas: Southern Methodist University. Their recommendations were ignored due to several factors, including the invasion of Spanish territory in east Texas by René Robert Cavelier, Sieur de La Salle who had sailed from Rochefort, France, on 1 August 1684, to seek the mouth of the Mississippi River by sea. He planned to settle near the Taensa Indian villages that lined Lake St. Joseph in Tensas Parish, Louisiana.
[28] Ibid.
[29] Joseph Luther to Clifford R. Caldwell. 30 August 2011.

The largest concentration of Catholic missions in North America, a string of five, were established along the San Antonio River in the 1700s. Most historians, as well as the early Spanish explorers themselves, have claimed that the missions were built primarily to foster Spain's expansion in the New World, and their influence north from Mexico. It is clear, however, that much of the motivation centered on the incessant quest for gold, silver and precious metals...made easier by the presence of local Indians who were pressed into service to perform the backbreaking work associated with the exploration and mission building.

Rarely were a people more harshly treated than the native Indians of Texas under Spanish rule. Spain's law provided for justice and humanity in the dealings with the Indians, but thousands of miles away in Texas these laws were largely ignored. Indians were reduced to slavery, or when free and given rights were viewed as inferior.[30]

In *Historical Tales: Spanish American* the author, Charles Morris, offers a stunning account of the seldom cited barbarity wrought upon the Indians of Texas:

> *The Spanish settlers had three terms that applied to their dealings with the Indians, the encomiendo, the mitad, and the repartimiento, each indicating a form of injustice. The conquerors divided the country between them, and the encomiendos were rights granted them to hold the Indians for a number of years as workers in their fields or their mines. Under these grants, the natives were converted into beasts of burden, and forced to do the hardest work without the least compensation. They were obliged to labor all day long under the burning tropical sun, to dive into the sea in search of pearls for their masters, or to toil buried from the light of day in the depths of the mines. It is not surprising that these miserable slaves, accustomed to a life of indolence and ease, perished as if exposed to a killing plague.*

Four of the missions (San Jose, San Juan, Concepcion, and Espada) were originally founded in East Texas. As the East

---

[30] Morris, Charles. 1904. *Historical Tales: Spanish American. Volume III.* Philadelphia, Pennsylvania: J.B. Lippincott Co.

Texas missions succumbed to drought, malaria, and French incursions they were relocated to San Antonio. San Antonio de Valero Mission was established 1 May 1718, as the Spanish created the Presidio of San Antonio de Béxar and the attached civil settlement…present-day San Antonio. After three moves from its original location west of San Pedro Creek, the San Antonio mission was placed at its present site in 1724. The earliest buildings did not survive. The parts that exist today were begun in 1727, when the stone convent was built. The existing chapel, the Alamo Shrine, was begun during the 1750s.

After the Mexican War of Independence from Spain (1810-1821) the province of Texas and the land surrounding Fort McKavett fell into Mexican hands. On 3 August 1830, John Charles Beales (1804-1878) married María Dolores Soto y Saldaña, the widow of Richard Exter. Exter was an English merchant and land speculator who had left María and their infant daughter his interests in two empresario contracts of 1826 and 1828 that encompassed roughly 48 million acres in eastern New Mexico, Texas, Oklahoma, and southeastern Colorado.[31] Exter had held these contracts jointly with Stephen Julian Wilson. Within weeks of the marriage Beales took over the management of these compacts. In New York, he transferred their interests to the Arkansas and Texas Land Company on 27 April 1831.

Next Beales entered the empresario sweepstakes on a grand scale for his own account. In an eight-month period in 1832 he persuaded officials of the state of Coahuila and Texas to grant him, and three different sets of partners, three empresario contracts for an estimated 55 million acres of land north of the Rio Grande. The first of these, dated 14 March 1832, authorized Beales and José Manuel Royuela to settle 200 families on the same tract originally granted Stephen Julian Wilson in 1826. The second, issued on 1 May 1832, permitted the so-called Mexican Company (Beales and three Mexican

---

[31] An empresario was a land agent or land contractor. Under the system used by the Mexican government as a means of colonization, some of the Texas empresarios were: Stephen F. Austin, John Beales, Samuel May Williams, Green DeWitt, Martin De Leon, Haden Edwards, Sterling C. Robertson, James Power, James Hewetson, John McMullen, James McGloin, and Arthur G. Wavell.

partners) to locate 450 families on 2 million acres in two parcels lying between the Colorado and Guadalupe rivers that had been granted to Green DeWitt in 1825 and Benjamin Rush Milam in 1826. The third, dated 9 October 1832, permitted Beales and Dr. James Grant to settle 800 families on 8 million acres in two separate tracts. One tract lay between the Rio Grande and the Nueces, the other including that portion of the 1826 grant to John Lucius Woodbury and Joseph Vehlein lying east of the 100th meridian.

In addition to his role in securing these empresario contracts, Beales appears to have masterminded the actions of his wife and eight other Mexican citizens, each of whom, on 16–18 October, purchased in fee simple an eleven-league tract of "unoccupied land" in the Department of Monclova. In the week after acquiring title, each of the purchasers gave Beales a power of attorney granting him the authority to sell or transfer title to his respective purchase.

Armed with these authorizations, and those of his partners in the empresario contracts, Beales again approached New York speculators. Between April 1833 and January 1835 he was intimately involved in the scheming of the directors of three land companies to which he sold his interests in the lands over which he had acquired control in 1832. To the New Arkansas and Texas Land Company, established in 1833, he ceded one-half of his interest in the Beales-Royuela grant. To the Rio Grande and Texas Land Company he deeded a large part of the Beales-Grant contract and the nine eleven-league purchases. To the Colorado and Red River Land Company he transferred control over approximately one-half of the land in the Mexican Company contract lying between the Colorado and Guadalupe rivers. In addition he concluded agreements with a number of individuals, including John Woodward, to whom he passed title to 4 million acres in different grants.

During the same period Beales spent much time and money recruiting settlers for a colonization project located between the Rio Grande and Nueces. In the end he was able to persuade fewer than 100 persons to settle at Dolores, the village named for his wife that he established in the area of present Kinney County on Las Moras Creek, eighteen miles above its junction with the Rio Grande.[32] Beales's attempt to plant a colony in that dry region came to an end when the colonists abandoned the site after the outbreak of the Texas Revolution.

From 1836 until his death in 1878, Beales sporadically fought in the courts and the legislative halls of the United States and Texas to validate his claims to lands in Texas and adjoining states. For the most part, neither judges nor legislators looked favorably on his petitions or his suits. His heirs were able to salvage only a fraction of the millions of acres to which he once had laid claim. After his death their titles to the eleven-league purchases in Southwest Texas were upheld by the courts.

Beales's dreams of gaining great wealth from his land grants were not fulfilled. In the absence of his journals and financial records, it is impossible to estimate how much he received from the transfer of his interests to the land companies. The total must have been considerable, if, as reported, the Rio Grande and Texas Land Company paid him as much as $100,000 for a portion of his interests in several grants.

The Fisher-Miller Land Grant, made by the Republic of Texas on 7 June 1842, is the next step in the line of ownership of the land upon which Fort McKavett is situated. The grant was

---

[32] On 11 November 1833, the *Amos Wright* sailed from New York for Texas with fifty-nine men, women, and children aboard. The group were under the command of John Charles Beales and had embarked on the journey to form a colony backed by the Rio Grande and Texas Land Company. From 1830 to 1832 Beales and other contractors had received several colonial grants totaling more than fifty million acres that lie in western Texas, eastern New Mexico, and the Rio Grande valley. On 1 May and 9 October 1832, Beales and James Grant acquired two tracts and obligated themselves to settle 800 families in the region between the Rio Grande and the Nueces Rivers. They set up a joint stock company to promote their venture.

The first colonists landed at Copano Bay on 12 December 1833, and journeyed in ox wagons to their destination at Las Moras Creek, a short distance down the Rio Grande from Presidio del Rio Grande and a few miles up the creek from its confluence with the river.

See - Lucy Lee Dickson, Speculation of John Charles Beales in Texas Lands (M.A. thesis, University of Texas, 1941). Raymond Estep, "The First Panhandle Land Grant," *Chronicles of Oklahoma* 36 (Winter 1958–59). Mary Virginia Henderson, "Minor Empresario Contracts for the Colonization of Texas, 1825–1834," *Southwestern Historical Quarterly* 31, 32 (April, July 1928). Carl Coke Rister, *Comanche Bondage: Dr. John Charles Beales's Settlement of La Villa de Dolores on Las Moras Creek in Southern Texas of the 1830s* (Glendale, California: Clark, 1955).

renewed on 1 September 1843, resulted from a petition made by Henry Francis Fisher, Burchard Miller, and Joseph Baker on 8 February 1842, to be permitted to settle 1,000 immigrant families of German, Dutch, Swiss, Danish, Swedish, and Norwegian ancestry in Texas under the auspices of the San Saba Colonization Company. The grant included more than three million acres between the Llano and Colorado rivers that had originally been a part of the Grant and Beales grant.[33]

The original contract allowed the introduction of 600 families and single men. Fisher and Miller did not succeed in colonizing the grant within the allotted time and took advantage of a legislative amendment passed on 6 January 1844, which extended the deadline. The amendment also increased the number of settlers to 6,000 families and single men. After seeking and obtaining the title of Texas consul to Bremen, Fisher went to Germany to promote colonization. On 26 June 1844, he sold an interest in the contract to the Adelsverein (the Society for the Protection of German Immigrants in Texas).[34]

---

[33] Citing - Estep, Raymond. "BEALES, JOHN CHARLES," *Handbook of Texas Online*.
Also see - Dickson, Lucy Lee Dickson. 1941. *Speculation of John Charles Beales in Texas Lands*. M.A. Thesis. University of Texas.
Estep, Raymond. "The First Panhandle Land Grant," *Chronicles of Oklahoma* 36. Winter 1958–1959.
Henderson, Mary Virginia. "Minor Empresario Contracts for the Colonization of Texas, 1825–1834," *Southwestern Historical Quarterly* 31, 32. April, July 1928.
Rister, Carl Coke. 1955. *Comanche Bondage: Dr. John Charles Beales's Settlement of La Villa de Dolores on Las Moras Creek in Southern Texas of the 1830s*. Glendale, California: Clark

[34] In 1842, a group of twenty-one German nobles met to deliberate a plan to settle Texas. Two years later they formed the Society for the Protection of German Immigrants in Texas, also known as the Adelsverein. Counts Ludwig Joseph von Boos-Waldeck and Victor August of Leiningen set out to explore and acquire land in Texas and to determine the necessary provisions for settlement. Boos-Waldeck named the land they bought Nassau Farm, which is presently located in Fayette County. Prince Karl of Solms-Braunfels, the first commissioner general, lived in Texas and provided for the immigrants that arrived. The Adelsverein's goals were commercial. Promoters aimed to open up new trade markets and amass natural resources from the land for Germany. The same year, Henry Francis Fisher and Burchard Miller landed a grant situated inside the Llano and Colorado Rivers. Members of the Adelsverein collaborated with them to colonize the

On 30 December 1845, Fisher and Miller sold their rights in the grant to the society. As a stipulation of the sale Fisher was appointed to the society's colonial committee. Along with the rights to the grant, the society had the responsibility to settle the area and take over any expenses accrued by the San Saba Colonization Company. The grant actually received few colonists from the society, which made only five small settlements; of the five, only Castell survived. Many of the settlers moved to New Braunfels or Fredericksburg and subsequently sold the grants they had received in the Fisher-Miller tract.[35] As a result of the failure of the Fisher-Miller project the land reverted back to the state of Texas.[36]

Less than a decade later Fort McKavett was established within the boundaries of the failed Fisher-Miller project. A 640 acre section of land was patented by Judge M.A. Dooley under a Third Class Headrights certificate (Survey No. 304) on 28 September 1854. Dooley leased the site to the government for $600 a year, with a twenty year lease being signed in December 1855. Dooley eventually sold the land to Joshua D. Robinson on 15 November 1858 for $4,000 and continued the lease arrangement.[37]

The Village of Fort McKavett

Fisher-Miller Grant. The Adelsverein promised the settlers comfortable and spacious ships, reasonable travel charges, free transportation to the settlement, and ways to find shelter and make a living. The Adelsverein's visions were idealistic, and organizers were overwhelmingly unprepared for the conditions awaiting their settlers. Lack of financial and administrative foresight haunted the Adelsverein, as immigrants found themselves stranded, often without adequate shelter, in a unfamiliar land.
See - Oommen, Sheena. *"Hin' nach Texas!* - Off to Texas!" Unpublished Manuscript. Undated.

[35] Rudolph L. Biesele, *The History of the German Settlements in Texas, 1831–1861* (Austin: Von Boeckmann-Jones, 1930; rpt. 1964). Solon Ollie Loving, A History of the Fisher-Miller Land Grant from 1842–1860 (M.A. thesis, University of Texas, 1934).

[36] On 29 December 1845 President James K. Polk signed the documents making Texas the twenty-eighth member of the United States of America, thus the land upon which Fort McKavett would soon be built lie within the boundaries of the newly formed State of Texas.

[37] Menard County Land Deed Records. Menard County, Texas. Volume I, pp 129-199. *Abstract of All Original Texas Land Titles.* 8 Volumes.

The tiny village of Fort McKavett is located at the intersection of farm roads 864 and 1674, twenty miles southwest of the town of Menard in southwestern Menard County. The community of civilians grew in the early 1850s alongside the military post, which was then known as Camp San Sabá. Originally the town, which was situated about a mile north of the post itself, was supposed to be named Lehnesburg in honor of a German merchant. Regrettably, citizenry of the day chose the uncomplimentary name "Scabtown" instead. Due to a decline in warfare with local Indian tribes the fort was closed in 1859. A handful of citizens remained in the area. Most chose to remove to more protected regions of the state.

Throughout the course of the Civil War, Indian depredations from Comanche and Kiowa Indians escalated. The small force of Texas Rangers who had been charged with the defense of the frontier were woefully understaffed and unable to beat back the constant raids and seemingly endless stream of cattle and horse theft.[38] In 1869, the Army reopened Fort McKavett as a military post when hostilities between local Comanche Indians and the settlers increased. From 1868 to 1883, Fort McKavett served as a major supply depot providing food and provisions for most of the military campaigns, scientific and mapping explorations in the region. It was also acted as a re-supply station for other military forts in West Texas.

---

[38] Texas has had its share of lawlessness. Starting in the 1820s the chief deterrent to crime in this multimillion-acre territory was a small group of lawmen who would later become known as the Texas Rangers. Stephen F. Austin organized two companies in 1823 "for the common defense." In 1835 the provisional government authorized a "ranging company" of twenty-five rangers. Later, that number was increased to a total of three companies consisting of fifty-six men each. Throughout the Republic period ranger units repelled Indian attacks and beat back invasions by bandits from Mexico. Often these companies of rangers were activated for only short periods, and disbanded after the crisis. Although their efforts were valiant, their numbers were still few. Increased immigration to Texas brought with it greater challenges, and further squeezed the Native American population whose ancestral lands were being settled by Anglo pioneers and homesteaders. Raiding parties of Mexican bandits from the south, often augmented by hostile Indians, pushed over the border at will, pillaging along the Rio Grande River.

Texans claimed that the federal government was not dedicating sufficient resources to the state, but in fact roughly twenty-five percent of the entire U.S. Army was based in Texas after the Civil War. A persistent shortage of mounted troops exacerbated the army's difficulties. In spite of these shortfalls, the frontier forts played an enormous part in Texas history. They were a haven from danger on the frontier for many travelers and the center of commerce from which many communities grew. From 1849 to 1900, the army disbursed roughly $70 million in Texas, a huge sum by any measure.[39]

Fort McKavett – circa 1880s
Photo courtesy of the University of Texas, Austin

Revived by the return of the troops, the civilian community at Fort McKavett began to grow again. Countless changes would occur over the coming decades. The town adopted a less obnoxious name, and by 1880 boasted a school, a church, and a variety of shops.

---

[39] Menard County Historical Society. 1982. *Menard County History-An Anthology*. San Angelo, Texas: Anchor. Vertical Files, Dolph Briscoe Center for American History. University of Texas at Austin.

Schoolhouse at Fort McKavett – circa 1880s
Photo courtesy of the Fort McKavett State Historical Site

Village of Fort McKavett – circa 1960
Photo courtesy of the Fort McKavett State Historical Site

The Military Outpost – Fort McKavett...

As for the history of the actual military fort called Fort McKavett, it was originally christened Camp San Saba, and was established by troops of the 8th U.S. Infantry in March 1852.

From the time at which Mission Santa Cruz de San Saba was plundered and destroyed in 1758, and the associated military outpost at Presidio San Luis de las Amarillas was abandoned in June 1771, there was little documented travel through the region surrounding present day Fort McKavett. James and Rezin Bowie passed through, and may have rediscovered the old silver mine that was once associated with the presidio (This topic is covered in a subsequent chapter). It was not until Baron John O. Meusebach trekked to the San Saba in January 1847 to negotiate with the Indians that any real attention was paid to the territory.[40] On 1 March 1849 Captain William Henry Chase Whiting and fifteen seasoned soldiers and guides made a foray into the area and camped at the headsprings of the river near where two Indian trails crossed. As fate would have it, their campsite was near where Fort McKavett was eventually established.[41]

As cited earlier, its purpose was to protect advancing settlers and serve as a rest stop for west bound immigrants. In search of a better route west, veteran Texas Ranger and surveyor John Coffee "Jack" Hays conducted an ill-fated exploration from San Antonio in 1848 that failed miserably. Hays led a combined force of men up the Llano River to Comanche Creek, then followed the James River and the north fork of the Nueces River over to Las Moras, a tributary of the Rio Grande. Hays' party finally reached a wide river bordered by cliffs and gorges that the Indians called the Puerce, which Hays named "Devil's River." The group reached the Pecos River on 26 September. They had gone only 418 miles in one month. As they wandered through the dry and rugged country west of the Pecos their

---

[40] Sullivan, Jerry M.. 1981. *Fort McKavett, A Texas Frontier Post*. Lubbock, Texas: Texas Parks and Wildlife. pp 5-6.
[41] Whiting, William Henry Chase. 1938. "Journal of William Henry Chase Whiting." *Exploring Southwest Trails*. Volume 7 of *Southwest Historical Series*. Edited by Ralph P. Bieber and Leroy C. Hafen. Glendale, California: Arthur C. Clarke. pp 255-256.

food ran out and water became scarce. By 9 October 1848, party member Samuel Maverick noted that they were "eating mustang meat." When after nine days they finally staggered into a small Mexican village on the Rio Grande named San Carlos they had been out of rations for twelve days and reduced to eating grass, rattlesnakes, skunks, panthers, and finally their own pack mules. In spite of the fact that they were now only 150 miles from accomplishing their mission and reaching El Paso, the group purchased enough food to make it to Fort Leaton (present day Presidio) and decided to return home. They could have traveled the remaining distance to El Paso, all by means of established wagon roads, in less than a week.

Hays's excursion was followed the next year by the more successful venture of fellow Texas Ranger, John S. "Rip" Ford, and U.S. Indian agent Robert Neighbors. Their effort began north of Austin and proceeded west, following the Concho River from its confluence with the Colorado, into the Trans-Pecos region, then west to El Paso. The Ford-Neighbors expedition returned by way of the Concho, San Saba, and Llano rivers, then through Fredericksburg and into San Antonio.

Not wishing to be outdone, the U.S. Army mounted its own expedition, paralleling the path of Ford and Neighbors. Lieutenants' William H.C. Whiting and William F. Smith left San Antonio and traveled through Fredericksburg to the San Saba River, then west to the Trans-Peco in January 1850. When they returned, Whiting recommended locating a garrison of mounted troops at old Presidio San Luis de las Amarillas. Lieutenant Whiting's 25 March 1850 report talks about the area around the location of present day Menard and Fort McKavett:

To know us, they must be made to feel us; and I can conceive of no better plan for this end than the disposition of two thousand mounted men upon the frontier, of which a garrison of two hundred may be placed on Red river, five, hundred on the Brazos, three hundred at the old San Saba fort, (a locality peculiarly eligible,) three hundred at Las Moras, and seven hundred at Preidio del Norte. The old San Saba fort, in the beautiful and luxuriant valley of the river of that name, is particularly eligible. One of the emigrant routes to California passes by it. It is situated with peculiar advantages for scouting to and from the settlements, and detecting the advance or retreat of predatory bands. It is the point once occupied by the Spanish garrison, whose work still remains, at once a lesson and a warning. From this point the scouts may scour the country traversed by the Indians in their descents to the lower country. To the westward pass those large bands of Comanches which, secure in the recesses of the Sierra Madre and the Bolson de Mapimi, carry on such extensive forays in the Mexican States, returning with incredible numbers of horses and mules.

On 16 December 1851, Brevet Major General Persifor Smith, commanding U.S. Army forces in Texas, ordered the construction of a post on the San Saba "at the headsprings of that river near the El Paso road."[42] The initial selection of building site proved unsatisfactory. The 8th Infantry Regiment arrived at the headwaters in March 1852, and established camp as ordered.[43] The site was on a small hill near a pond, but the camp was soon moved two miles downstream when the lagoon became stagnant.

Initially the new location was referred to as the "Camp on the San Saba" or "Post on the San Saba." In October, it was renamed Camp McKavett. Not long after the name was changed to Fort McKavett, in honor of Captain Henry McKavett of the 8th Infantry.[44]

---

[42] General Order 95. Eighth Military District, 16 December 1851. RG 94. National Archives.

[43] The 8th had originally been ordered to Camp Johnston on the Concho, but on 16 February 1852 General Smith ordered them to San Sabá. General Order 11. Eighth Military District, 16 February 1852. RG 94. National Archives.

[44] Captain Henry McKavett had served meritoriously in the Mexican War. The gallant Captain McKavett, 8th infantry, was killed at the Battle of Monterey on 21 September 1846. He was the only officer killed in the conflict that day. McKavett, who was from New York, applied to West Point in July 1829. It is unclear if he was admitted. He listed his age as fifteen years two months at the time of that application, making his year of birth circa 1814. See - National Archives and Records Administration (NARA). Washington, D.C.. Name Index to U.S. Military Academy Cadet Application Papers, 1805-1866. Microfilm Serial M688. Microfilm Roll 1.

By September 1835 McKavett was a 2nd Lieutenant and was stationed at Fort Gibbon, Oklahoma Territory. See - National Archives and Records Administration (NARA). Washington, D.C.; Returns from U.S. Military Posts, 1800-1916. Microfilm Serial M617. Microfilm Roll 404. By September 1838 McKavett had been promoted to the rank of 1st Lieutenant, and was

At the outset five companies of the 8th Infantry were assigned to the post. Construction soon began on permanent structures, which included five infantrymen's barracks, several kitchens (initially used as officers quarter's), a hospital, and a quartermaster's storehouse. The buildings were neatly arranged around a square parade ground.

Each of the five companies was responsible for building its own quarters. Limestone was quarried from a site near the post for building foundations and walls. Mortar was made locally as well, probably in the original kiln located a short distance from the new site. Locally grown oak and pecan logs were felled and used for the construction of some buildings in a picket post, style.[45] Improvements were made through the mid-1850s. A two-story quarters for the commanding officer and one-story barracks for other officers and adjutant's office were added. A new guardhouse, a new bakery and kitchens, and a laundry quarters were also built.

At the beginning Fort McKavett was garrisoned by one company of mounted infantry consisting of forty-six men with only thirty serviceable horses. Early on, one of the most significant problems encountered by the post commander was that of the overflowing guardhouse. Many of the men had been imprisoned for months, awaiting sentence or trial. [46]

Feeding the troops was costly. The monthly expenditure for fresh beef and whiskey totaled $400. Rations, in total, ran twenty-one and one half cents per ration.[47]

---

stationed at the Madison Barracks in New York. See - National Archives and Records Administration (NARA). Washington, D.C.. Returns from U.S. Military Posts 1800-1916. Microfilm Serial. M617. Microfilm Roll. 721.

In 1842 McKavett was assigned to Brooke Fort in Florida. By that time he had been promoted to the rank of Captain, McKavett remained with the 8th Infantry in Florida until June 1845 – prior to his duty in the Mexican War.

[45] As was the case with many forts on the frontier such as Terrett and McKavett, at first the troops and officers quarters did not have lumber for floors or doors, nor glass for windows. Materials were later purchased by the government or by the troops and officers themselves and transported from nearby civilian supply centers like Fredericksburg.

[46] Crimmins, M.L. Editor. "Notes and Documents, W.G. Freeman's Report on the Eighth Military District." *Southwest History Quarterly*. Volume 53. 1949. Volume 54. 1950.

[47] Ibid. p 313.

When Fort McKavett was established the Model 1842 Musket was the standard long-arm of the United States Infantry. Companies D, E, H, and part of Company F of the 8th Infantry were equipped with this weapon, as were Companies C & E of the 1st Infantry. The Model 1842 followed the basic design of every U.S. produced musket from 1795 forward. It was the first U.S. musket to use a percussion cap, and the last smoothbore weapon produced by government armories. Production began in 1844, and guns were first issued during the Mexican-American War. The Model 1842 saw service as late as the Civil War.[48]

Colonel Charles May's 2nd Dragoons arrived at the fort in February 1854, replacing the 8th Infantry who had opened the fort. In October 1857 the 1st relieved the 2nd Dragoons, who were sent to Fort Riley, Kansas, and remained until the post closed in 1859.

Along with the 8th came the regimental band, which brought a scarce and needed bit of culture to the post.[49] Unfortunately the band moved on to Fort Chadbourne in March 1853, leaving Fort McKavett silent but for the howl of the odd coyote or inebriated soldier stumbling back from a night of celebrating. Episcopal minister John Fish arrived about the time of the band's exit, however. He took over duties as chaplain and schoolteacher.

Most of the military activities mounted against hostile Indians were confined to scouts and brief excursions. The first punitive expedition took place in July 1852. Once the Dragoons took over forays into the field were made easier. Starting in about June 1854 troops remained in the field much of the time. In 1856 several bands of Indians agreed to be placed on a reservation near Fort Belknap, which temporarily paused scouting parties. In May 1856 depredations flared up again, and two detachments of infantry were ordered to deploy along the Llano River and Kickapoo Creek.[50] A detachment of twenty-

---

[48] *Fort McKavett Gazette*. Volume 8 Number 2. February 2009.
[49] Sullivan, Jerry M.. 1981. *Fort McKavett, A Texas Frontier Post*. Lubbock, Texas: Texas Parks and Wildlife. p 16.
[50] Special Order 53. Department of Texas. 5 May 1856. RG 94. National Archives.

five soldiers was sent to the old site of Fort Terrett, which had been abandoned a year earlier.

When the Penateka Comanche withdrew from the Hill Country in the late 1850s, to either the Clear Fork reservation or the Indian Territory beyond the Red River, Fort McKavett was ordered abandoned on 5 February 1859. That order was executed on 22 March 1859, leaving the protection of Texans living in the San Sabá Valley to settlers and the tiny band of Texas Rangers.

In a report of date 1853, Assistant Surgeon S. Wylie Crawford stated that five deaths had occurred at the Fort in 1852 - one from scurvy, one from suicide, two from dysentery, and one from a pulmonary ailment. No listing of deaths during the period from 1 January 1853 to 22 March 1859 has been uncovered. One of the men who died in 1852 was Christian Weaver, a member of Company F, 8th Infantry. His group arrived at Camp McKavett on 14 March 1852. Weaver died seventeen days later. His grave was probably one of the many unmarked and thus not moved to San Antonio.

Early Map of Fort McKavett
Photo courtesy of the Fort McKavett State Historical Site

The fort did not remain completely vacated during the Civil War years as many have reported. Robert Robinson, a member of the family that owned the land upon which the fort was built, occupied the commanding officers quarters.[51] Several other families lived in assorted buildings, cow pens and barns.[52]

On 18 February 1861, seventeen days after Texas seceded from the Union, General David E. Twiggs, Commander of the Military Department of Texas, surrendered the stores and the seventeen military outposts of the United States forces in Texas to the Confederacy.[53] The remaining federal troops began their march to Indianola to board awaiting ships for their departure from the Lone Star State. Not all made it to the coast before the established May deadline however. Along the way 320 soldiers of the 8th Infantry Regiment under the command of Brevet Colonel I.V.D. Reeve encountered a group of 1,350 Texas State Troops near San Antonio. Facing this superior force, six companies of the 8th (B,E,F,H,I and K) surrendered at the Battle of Adam's Hill, near San Antonio, on 9 May 1861. They were taken prisoner. The captive Federal soldiers were held near Salado Creek, five miles west of San Antonio. In early September the prisoners were moved to Camp Verde, near Kerrville.[54]

The various companies of the 8th were divided amongst the former Federal outposts on the Texas frontier. On 18 September 1861 Confederate General P.O. Hébert, head of the Military Department of Texas, issued General Order No. 1 which stated that:

---

[51] Citing Sullivan, Jerry M.. 1981. *Fort McKavett, A Texas Frontier Post.* Lubbock, Texas: Texas Parks and Wildlife. p 25.
[52] Winslow, Edith Black. 1950. *In Those Days: Memories of the Edwards Plateau.* San Antonio, Texas: Naylor. p 11.
[53] Citing Cody Mobley. Manuscript on the Role of Fort McKavett during the American Civil War. Copy dated 27 September 2011. Also see - United States War Department. The war of the rebellion: a compilation of the records of the Union and Confederate armies. Series 2. Volume 1. p 12. Special Order No. 41.
[54] Citing Cody Mobley. Manuscript on the Role of Fort McKavett during the American Civil War. Copy dated 27 September 2011.

Colonel McColloch will order the removal of the prisoners from Camp Verde and place them for safety in detachments at the different posts in his command.

Accordingly, some of the 320 Union soldiers were marched to Fort McKavett in October 1861 where they were held for a six month period under guard by Company E, 1st Texas Mounted Rifles. Thus the old fort served as a temporary prisoner of war camp. All of the incarcerated Federal soldiers were enlisted men and non commissioned officers. The officers were kept in San Antonio. In April 1862 the prisoners were moved to Fort Mason. By November the fort was being used as a depot for redistribution of supplies coming from San Antonio.[55] That purpose continued through 1862.

By 1864 Fort McKavett was once again abandoned until 21 April 1865 when a force of 161 Texas State Troops under the command of John Henry Brown's camped at the old stronghold for two days on their way to Kickapoo Creek.[56] Brown's encampment was the last military occupation during the Civil War. On 26 May 1865, at New Orleans, Lieutenant General Simon Bolivar Buckner surrendered the army of the Trans-Mississippi on behalf of Confederate General Edmund Kirby Smith. For Texans the war was over. Most walked home.

About 2,000 were not yet ready to give up, however. They fled into Mexico, either one by one or in small groups. One larger body numbering about 300 was led by the resolute Kirby Smith, mounted on a mule, wearing a calico shirt and silk kerchief, sporting a revolver strapped to his hip and a shotgun on his saddle.

The 1st Texas Mounted Rifles had been on campaign since March of 1861. These men were the first regiment that Texas created during the Civil War, and the commission to form the regiment was the first issued by the Confederate Government. The men that composed this outfit, in part, had experience in the Texas Ranger Ranging Companies of the 1850s. By

---

[55] Citing Cody Mobley. Manuscript on the Role of Fort McKavett during the American Civil War. Copy dated 27 September 2011.
[56] Ibid. Brown had left Camp Verde with 183 men, loosing twenty men along the way.

November 1861, attrition had begun to take a toll on the men of the 1st. Frequent patrols against the Lipan Apache and Comanche had reduced the once seventy to eighty man strong group to a mere fifty or sixty rugged survivors.

During much of the 1860s Indians pillaged at will. Incidents are numerous. A major raid took place on 6 August 1866 near Fort McKavett, when several hundred Kickapoos moved through the valley and made off with 15,000 head of livestock. Miraculously, only two settlers were killed during the affray.

Newspaper accounts of the era give insight into the extent of the Indian depredations in the region:

Galveston Daily News. 13 August 1868
A letter from Menardsville, Menard County, informs the San Antonio Herald that the Indians are in there on thieving expeditions. Fort McKavett, says the writer, is 23 miles above; plenty of soldiers, but nothing done to save us from Indian depredations.

Galveston Daily News. 22 March 1870
Seven hundred and fifty dollars reward in gold is offered by P. Field for the safe delivery at any point in the United States of Mrs. Dorothy Field, abducted by Indians from Menard County, on the San Saba River, four miles below Fort McKavett, Texas on February 27th.

Galveston Daily News. 27 August 1870
A Distressed Husband--Mr. P. Field of Menard County, writes to the San Antonio Herald, that he will give $1,200 in specie for the return of his wife, Dorothy Field, who was stolen by Indians some time ago.

Galveston Daily News. 15 April 1871
Adjutant General's Office,
State of Texas,
Austin, 8 April 1871
Report of Indian depredations committed in Menard County, from 1 January 1866 to 31 March 1871:
No. of persons killed………………………………..8
No. of persons wounded……………………….......2

No. of persons carried to captivity..................2
No. of horses and mules stolen..........…........619
No. of cattle killed and stolen.........…….....6,660
No. of houses burned.................……..……..1
Total value of property destroyed.......$101,430

These outrages were committed by the Kickapoo and Comanche tribes of Indians. Official: James Davidson, Adjutant General of Texas

Galveston Daily News. 6 August 1873
...There has been no fight with the Indians, and but one Indian killed, which was at Fort McKavett. He was a chief, as is to be seen by his outfit, which is here in San Antonio. It is uncertain which tribe he belonged to, but this will be determined in a few days as his hat and other articles have been sent to Fort Sill for that purpose.

Galveston Daily News. 20 November 1873
Colonel Napier, an old citizen of San Antonio, has just returned from McKavett, and from him we glean the following Indian items:
"Ten Indians pursued an agile old Mexican to his residence at Kickapoo Springs, about twenty-six miles from McKavett. They were thought to be Arizona Indians. This occurred about ten days ago. At Seven Mile Station sixteen miles west of Fredericksburg, another Mexican successfully evaded another bunch of social redskins. Again, at Taylor's ranch, or "Peg-Leg", where the first stage stand is, the first station this side of Menardville, several Indians attacked a small train, but were repulsed. They shot two mules, however. Buffalo had already made their appearance, and fine hunting was predicted....

Galveston Daily News. 30 April 1874
Gentlemen recently from Fort McKavett report that Indian depredations are more frequent and daring than ever. During the last three weeks upward of 200 head of horses have been stolen from Menard County. Last Saturday a party of ten Indians crossed the San Saba about seven miles from Fort

McKavett. The Indians are believed to be Mescaleros, Apaches, Comanches and Kiowas, from the reservation.

Galveston Daily News. 5 June 1875
The Sentinel says it is rumored that Mr. R.F. Tankersley and four other men were murdered by Indians on the road between Fort McKavett and Concho.

Galveston Daily News. 19 February 1878
Indians are reported raiding above Fort McKavett. Troops are in pursuit.

Finally, on 1 April 1868, Fort McKavett was reoccupied by Company A of the 4th Cavalry under the command of Brevet Lieutenant Colonel Eugene B. Beaumont. One source described the condition of the facility as being in an advanced state of dilapidation, "one mass of ruins" with only one habitable house.[57] The troops lived in tents while repairs and new construction took place.[58] Some historians have alleged that the arriving black troopers were poorly equipped, poorly armed and poorly mounted, claiming that this second class treatment was intentional, and racially motivated. Painstaking research on the part of the authors of *Black Regulars, 1866-1898* seems to prove otherwise, however, emphasizing that all regiments on the frontier, black and white, suffered from material shortages on occasion.[59] What is clear, however, is that many of the green recruits who arrived at Fort McKavett had little or no experience with firearms. Some had never held one in the hands before enlisting. As a result, extensive marksmanship training was conducted. Some soldiers were instructed to simply point the weapon at the distant geological feature called "Target Hill," located southeast of the fort, and fire.

Colonel George A. Gordon assumed command on 10 April 1868. He brought with him new troops. Company F of the 4th

---

[57] Dial, Steven. "The Post on the San Saba." *Texas Beyond History*. 30 June 2003
[58] *Fort McKavett and the Hill Country Frontier*. Steve Dial. Contributing Editor for *Texas Beyond History*. University of Texas at Austin.
[59] Dobak, William A. and Phillips, Thomas D. 2001. *Black Regulars, 1866-1898*. Norman, Oklahoma: University of Oklahoma Press.

Cavalry arrived on 17 April and Companies D, E and I made their appearance on 23 April. By the following spring, 15 March 1869 to be precise, the 38th Infantry and its controversial commanding officer Colonel Ranald Slidell Mackenzie came on the scene.[60,61]

The 38th was one of the army's six regiments having black enlisted personnel and white officers. It would be the first such unit to be headquartered at Fort McKavett, and its commander would go on to become one of the foremost Indian fighters of the post-Civil War army. On 1 September 1869 the 38th was combined with the 41st to create the 24th infantry, headquartered at Fort McKavett. The 9th Cavalry, another regiment of black enlisted men and white officers, was also garrisoned at Fort McKavett.[62,63]

---

[60] Ranald Slidell Mackenzie (27 July1840 – 19 January 1889) was a career army officer and general in the Union Army during the Civil War. Mackenzie also served with great distinction in the Indian Wars in Texas.

Mackenzie attended Williams College and later accepted a nomination to West Point. He graduated at the head of his class in 1862 and immediately joined the Union forces, which were already fighting in the Civil War. Commissioned a second lieutenant Mackenzie saw action at Second Bull Run, Antietam and Gettysburg. He was wounded at Jerusalem Plank Road during the siege of Petersburg. The injury cost him two of his fingers, and resulted in his peculiar byname "Bad Hand". By June 1864 Mackenzie had been promoted to the rank of Brevet Lieutenant Colonel for his bravery.

In July 1864, he was promoted to the rank of colonel. He saw distinguished service in several campaigns, including the Battle of Fort Stevens, Battle of Cedar Creek, Battle of Five Forks, the Appomattox Courthouse and the Shenandoah Valley Campaign. General Ulysses S. Grant described him as the army's most promising young officer.

After the Civil War, Mackenzie stayed in the army and reverted to his permanent rank of captain in the Army Corps of Engineers. Appointed colonel of the 41st U.S. Infantry in 1867, one of the Buffalo Soldiers regiments Mackenzie spent the rest of his career on the Frontier.

[61] Some sources have cited the 41st as black infantry unit first located at Fort McKavett.

[62] While Lieutenant Colonel William "Pecos Bill" Shafter was in command a diminutive 9th Cavalry Sergeant Emanuel Stance led a patrol from Fort McKavett. Stance directed his detachment of ten troopers in two engagements with Indian raiders on successive days in a fight called the Battle of Kickapoo Springs. Stance led three charges, two of them in the same action and all of them successful. He had fought in a total of five engagements in two years, a rarity for any soldier of the frontier army at that time. His record earned him the Medal of Honor – the first black soldier to

Mackenzie imported five civilian carpenters and six stonemasons who aided the soldiers of the 24th in making substantial improvement and expansion on the fort, which was soon considered to be one of the best in Texas. An absence of skilled labor, both indigenous as well as amongst the troops, was a problem in the rebuilding of the fort however. In 1869 the roster of civilian employees at Fort McKavett included one clerk, three masons, one wheelwright, six carpenters, and one post guide. The post guide at that time was J.E. Delong. He and his brother had started a ranch in the area of present Christoval, at the headwaters of the Lower Concho River. The total expenditure for civilian employees in July 1869 was $900. These men were provided with housing and food along with their monthly payment. In 1869, $900 was no small sum, but had to be paid to get skilled help on the frontier.[64]

---

achieve this distinction during the post Civil War period.
[63] Edited by Theophilus Frances Rodenbrough. Bvt. Brigadier General and William L. Haskin. Major, First Artillery. 1896. *The Army of the United States. Historical Sketches of Staff and Line With Portraits of General-in-Chief.* Maynard, Merril & Co. Entry reads as follows – "Under the Act of March 3, 1869, the 38th and 41st Regiments were consolidated and became the 24th Infantry, and as thus reëstablished has since continued in service. Under this reorganization Ronald S. Mackenzie became colonel, William R. Shafter, lieutenant colonel, and Henry C. Merriam, major. Of the captains assigned to the new regiment there are in active service at this writing, six, but two only serving in it; and of the twenty lieutenants there are also six, but four only remaining in it. A few of the enlisted men who served in the War of the Rebellion or in the 38th Of 41st Regiments may still be seen in its ranks.
The regiment was in Texas from 1869 to 1880 and at some time during that period the several companies were stationed at all or nearly all of the many posts and permanent camps in that great State."
[64] *Fort McKavett Gazette.* Volume 3 Number 6. June 2004.

Officers Quarters 7,8,9 &10 - Fort McKavett – Circa 1870
Photo courtesy of the Fort McKavett State Historical Site

Among the chores that were contracted out was the post's laundry. U.S. Army laundresses, who were often the wives of senior enlisted men, were given daily rations, quarters, fuel, bedding, and medical services. Their quarters were often substandard at best. The women who performed the laborious task of washing the post's soiled clothes and linens were both black and white, and children occasionally among their numbers. Until the final years at Fort McKavett the post did not have quarters for enlisted men's families, thus many wives became laundresses just to be able to stay with their husbands. At some western forts the laundry women were not predominantly spouses of troopers, with their ranks interspersed with "soiled doves" who plied their trade on the eager ranks of the post's enlisted men. Fort McKavett boasted twenty-eight Laundress Quarters on the north side of the facility, one on the south side, and five on the east side. Laundresses were paid $10-$12 per month, plus their rations and housing. They received additional pay "by the piece" for the clothing that they washed.[65]

Progress was slow. Mackenzie's stay at Fort McKavett got off to a bad start as well, when he clashed with General Joseph Jones Reynolds over the latter's role in contaminated grain shipments to the fort.[66] In spite of his allegations that he had evidence, which he called his "ace in the hole" Mackenzie lost the bout, and his records was forever clouded by the incident.[67]

Frank Eben Conrad was the sutler, or post trader, at Fort McKavett from 1868 to 1871. Conrad was born on 4 May 1842, at Rockford, Illinois. After his parents died he was taken to San Antonio, Texas, and reared by an aunt and uncle and was a clerk at his uncle's store at the outbreak of the Civil War. Conrad enlisted in Hood's Texas Brigade and served until the end of the conflict. When federal forces reoccupied Fort McKavett in 1868, Conrad was appointed post trader. In 1871 he sold his store to his clerk Samuel Wallick and won the bid to become the post trader at Fort Griffin, where he established an enviable reputation as a merchant. During the Indian campaigns from 1872 to 1875, Fort Griffin was Colonel Mackenzie's supply base, thus Conrad's store did a thriving business. At the conclusion of the Indian campaigns, Conrad's store remained in business and supplied buffalo hunters with guns, ammunition, and provisions of all sorts. He actively engaged in barter with the hunters, buying their hides and freighting them from the range. When traffic began along the Western Trail to Kansas Conrad's store was an important provisioning point on the trail. He later added a new store at Albany in order to get a major share of the drovers' trade. Conrad was also involved in the bone trade in later years before retiring in 1891. He committed suicide in Albany on 4 May 1892.[68]

The nearby civilian village called Scabtown was a collection of ramshackle buildings that were situated across the river from the post. Beyond the legitimate trade enterprises engaged in by the citizenry, the little town made available those contraband

---

[65] *Fort McKavett Gazette*. Volume 5 Number 9. September 2006.
[66] By mid 1877 grain supply to the fort came from local merchants Faltin & Schreiner, operating out of Kerrville and Junction City. *Galveston Daily News*. 13 July 1877.
[67] Nohl Jr., Lessing H. "Bad Hand:The Military Career of Ranald Slidell Mackenzie, 1871-1889." PhD Dissertation. University of New Mexico.
[68] *Fort McKavett Gazette*. Volume 4 Number 6. June 2005.

goods and assorted debaucheries that the fort's sutler was not permitted to provide. On balance Scabtown was probably no worse than most such encampments, populated by a mix of legitimate citizens seeking to engage in trade with the post and its inhabitants and a sprinkling of traditional "camp followers" consisting of card sharps and sporting women.[69] Life on the post could become boring, thus all manner of distraction was generally welcome. If not on patrol, the routine involved various work details as well as building and maintenance activities at the post. Only a few hours each weekday, and Sunday, was set aside for relaxation. As has been the case with soldiers since the beginning of time, excessive consumption of alcohol was one of the primary forms of relaxation. Its overuse often led to serious consequences for the troops. In terms of ethnicity, practically all of the soldiers were black. The 1870 census shows 191 black, 144 mulatto and one "white Negro" who had been born in England, making a total of 336 in all. The term "white Negro" in this instance was used by the census taker to categorize a US soldier named Levi Perkins who was of East Indian ancestry.[70] Perkins happened to be classically dark skinned, and had hair resembling a black man, thus he was able to gain entry into the ranks of the otherwise all Negro military unit.[71] Interestingly, although practically all were from southern states, none of the soldiers hailed from Texas. According to the 1870 census, the total population of Menard County was 667.[72] Soldiers and citizens were on a one to one ratio.

---

[69] Blevins Dictionary of the American West. 2001. One of the many terms for prostitute. The Westerner is fecund with names of things that interest him, so he has many expressions for the woman for sale: ceiling expert, hippy, crib girl, Cyprian, dance-hall girl, frail denizen, frail sister, girl [or ladies] of the line, girl of the night, horizontal worker, hurdy-gurdy girl, inmate of a house of ill fame, margarita, nymph du pave, nymph du prairie, painted cat, soiled dove, sport, sporting women, woman of evil name and fame. In the 1870s and 1880s, newspaper editors needed to talk about such matters, and propriety led to creativity."
[70] US Census. Census Year 1870. Census Place Menard, Texas . Roll M593_1594. Page 162A. Image 327. Family History Library Film 553093.
[71] Cody Mobley (Fort McKavett State Historical Site Collections/Exhibits Technician) to Clifford R. Caldwell. 27 September 2011.
[72] US Census. Census Year 1870. Census Place Menard, Texas. Roll M593_1594. Page 158. Image 319. Family History Library Film 553093.

The *Fort McKavett Gazette*, a valuable source of historical information on the old post that is published by the Friends of Fort McKavett, contains a wealth of interesting facts and interesting article. The gazette has been published since 2002.

Payday at Fort McKavett took place about once monthly and depended to some degree on weather and activity of the unit. After May 1872, trooper's longevity pay was withheld until discharge, with interest paid at a rate of 4%.[73]

- Sergeant Major $23.00
- Quartermaster Sergeant $23.00
- Chief Trumpeter $20.00
- Hospital Steward, 3rd Class $20.00
- Principal Musician $20.00
- Saddler Sergeant $22.00
- First Sergeant $22.00
- Duty Sergeant $17.00
- Corporal $15.00
- Blacksmith $15.00
- Farrier $15.00
- Trumpeter $13.00
- Private $13.00
- Saddler $15.00
- Hospital Steward, 1st Class $30.00
- Hospital Steward, 2nd Class $22.00
- Ordnance Sergeant $34.00
- Ordnance Private 1st Class $17.00
- Ordnance Private 2nd Class $13.00
- Engineer Private, 1st Class $17.00
- Engineer Private 2nd, Class $13.00
- Signal Corps Private, 1st Class $17.00
- Signal Corps Private, 2nd Class $13.00
- Mechanics Extra Pay $0.35/Day

Also see - Sullivan, Jerry M.. 1981. *Fort McKavett, A Texas Frontier Post.* Lubbock, Texas: Texas Parks and Wildlife. p 45.

[73] *Fort McKavett Gazette*. Volume 1 Number 6. November 2002.

- Laborers Extra Pay $0.25/Day
- 3rd Year Service Longevity Pay $1.00/Month
- 4th Year Service Longevity Pay $2.00/Month
- 5th Year Service Longevity Pay $3.00/Month

A change in regiments took place in 1879. The Buffalo Soldiers, who during the post Civil War Reconstruction Era were somewhat unpopular among many of the populace, were replaced with white cavalry troops. According to the *Galveston Daily News* of 13 July 1879 "The town, which during the time the 10th [cavalry] was here was dull and stupid is now transformed" citing that "…things have improved both physically and morally" with "good order" being one of the transformations. The tone of the foregoing account provides some insight into the still racially biased rural south.

One of the replacement units, the 22nd, only remained at Fort McKavett for a brief time however. Headquarters of the 22nd Infantry Regiment arrived at the fort in May 1879. When the 4th Cavalry was ordered to Sioux territory in November 1879 the 22nd was dispatched to Fort Clark. A few companies of the 22nd stayed at Fort McKavett until January of 1881, when the 1st Infantry Regiment replaced them. The 1st was on its way to Fort Davis and remained at McKavett for only a couple of months.[74] Captain Oskaloosa M. Smith filed the following, uninspiring report of the units activities on 15 November 1895:[75]

> In 1879 the regiment was ordered to the Department of Texas and started for that department in April. While en route, on account of some Indian difficulties, Companies D, E, F and K, under command of Colonel Hough, were ordered to take station at Fort Gibson, Indian Territory, and the other companies would no doubt have been stopped also, but they were in advance and had already reached Texas. The colonel, lieutenant-colonel and Companies B, C, H and I were assigned to Fort McKavett, A to Fort Griffin. Fort McKavett was made sad and gloomy July 4th, by the death of Capt. T. H. Fisher, a very

---

[74] *Fort McKavett Gazette.* Volume 5 Number 3. March 2006.
[75] Edited by Theophilus Frances Rodenbrough. Bvt. Brigadier General and William L. Haskin. Major, First Artillery. 1896. *The Army of the United States. Historical Sketches of Staff and Line With Portraits of General-in-Chief.* Maynard, Merril & Co. Account of Captain Oskaloosa M. Smith

popular officer in the regiment. Early in the summer Company E went to Vinita, I. T., and K to Coffeeville, Kansas, where they remained until October, for the purpose of keeping boomers out of Oklohoma [Oklahoma] and to protect the inhabitants from the robbers who infested that part of the country.

By the time of the 1880 census the ethnicity of the force had changed drastically. Of the 181 men stationed at Fort McKavett in 1880 none were black, 84 were foreign born, with the majority having come from Ireland, Germany and England. The last of the black troops had departed in November 1879. There were also sixteen wives of soldiers at the post in 1880. There had been none ten years earlier.

Relations between the black troops at the fort and the townspeople was not always the best, in spite of the fact that most of the town's populace was also black...including the constable. During the first incident the peace officer became involved in a fracas with two unruly troopers, one of whom he shot through the mouth during the struggle.[76] On 28 February 1877 gunfire and mayhem broke out when a group of Kimble County men arrived in town and attempted to free two friends named Ben Anderson and Jimmy Love who had been locked up for stealing horses. After a confusing exchange of gunfire the pair were detained at the fort overnight and sent packing, sans friends, back to Kimble County in the morning.[77]

2nd Lieutenant Henry Kirby, who was stationed with the 10th Infantry at Fort McKavett, wrote an account describing the troubles at the post in 1877. He indicated that during the previous year, 1876, "There have been five persons shot and killed within less than three-quarters of a mile of the post since I arrived, and it is said to be rather quiet compared to what it was some years ago." Another report chronicled an episode in which four men and a little girl were killed in a shoot-out at Scabtown.

On the evening of 1 January 1878, Ben Johnson and George Stevenson, who were serving as teamsters for the

---

[76] Sullivan, Jerry M.. 1981. *Fort McKavett, A Texas Frontier Post*. Lubbock, Texas: Texas Parks and Wildlife. p 39.
[77] Ibid. p 40.

rangers, left the Texas Ranger camp near the post to attend a dance in town. Stevenson borrowed a pistol from a Private McCarty. Once in town, the two teamsters were confronted by a group of local men who were black soldiers from the Tenth Cavalry stationed at the fort. After a bit of a fracas occurred, the black troopers took the borrowed revolver from the freighters. The two teamsters returned to the ranger camp and reported the theft of McCarty's pistol. Lieutenant Reynolds told Sergeant McGee and Private McCarty to go back to town and get the gun. They did so.

As McGhee and McCarty approached the dance hall the men closed the door and denied the rangers entry. McGhee ordered the men to return the pistol and surrender. He covered the front door while McCarty guarded the back door. Anticipating further trouble, George Stevenson was sent back to the camp to get Lieutenant Reynolds. Reynolds returned with privates Tom Gillespie and Dick Harrison. The men in the dance hall again refused to surrender...this time to the intrepid Reynolds. He then ordered the dance hall cleared of all women and gave the men five minutes to surrender.

The mood inside the dance hall began to transform as the women started screaming and the anxiety of the men grew. One of the fellows poked McCarty's gun out through a window, muzzle first, and said, "Here...come get your damned pistol." As McCarty stepped forward and gripped the gun the man holding it pulled the trigger. The bullet struck McCarty just below the heart, inflicting a serious wound.[78]

The rangers opened fire, killing three men. One man managed to escape in the midst of the mayhem as a mass of humanity poured forth from the little dance hall like rats from a sinking ship.

McCarty lingered until 1:20 a.m. on 2 January, when he finally expired. He is buried at the Fort McKavett cemetery.[79]

---

[78] Caldwell, Clifford R. and DeLord, Ron. 2011. *Texas Lawmen 1835-1899, The Good and the Bad*. Charleston, South Carolina: The History Press. pp 334-335.

[79] McCarty was born circa 1851. He had first enlisted as a private in Company F on 4 June 1875 and later re-enlisted in Company A on 10 September 1877. McCarty's tombstone has his date of death inscribed as 31 December 1877 - New Years Eve.

Texas Ranger Captain James Buchanan Gillett thought that the foregoing incident was significant enough to record it in his book *Six Years With The Texas Rangers*, published in 1921. Although Gillett's account differs slightly from other more historically accurate versions, it is none-the-less reflective of the contemptuous attitude of the day with regard to blacks:

Shortly afterward Reynolds selected Sergeant McGee, Tom Gillespie, Dick Harrison, and Tim McCarthy and made a scout into Menard County. He also had with him his Negro cook, George, to drive his light wagon. On the return toward Bear Creek the scout camped for the night at Fort McKavett. At that time each frontier post had its chihuahua, or scab town, a little settlement with gambling halls, saloons, etc., to catch the soldiers' dollars. At Fort McKavett were many discharged soldiers, some of them Negroes from the Tenth Cavalry. These blacks had associated with white gamblers and lewd women until they thought themselves the equals of white men, and became mean and overbearing. On this particular night these Negro ex-soldiers gave a dance in scab town, and our Negro, George, wanted to go. He was a light mulatto, almost white, but well thought of by all the boys in the company. He obtained Lieutenant Reynolds' permission to attend the dance, and borrowed Tim McCarthy's pistol to carry to it. When George arrived at the dance hall the ex-soldiers did not like his appearance, as he was allied with the rangers, whom they despised. They jumped on George, took his pistol and kicked him out of the place. The boys were all in bed when George returned and told McCarthy that the Negroes at the dance hall had taken his pistol from him.

Lieutenant Reynolds was sleeping nearby and heard what George said. He raised up on his elbow and ordered Sergeant McGee to go with McCarthy and George and get the pistol. The Negroes saw McGee coming and, closing the door, defied him to enter the dance hall.

McGee was cool and careful. He advised the Negroes to return the pistol, but they refused, saying they would kill the first white-livered SOB that attempted to enter the house. The sergeant then stationed himself at the front door, ordered McCarthy to guard the back entrance of the place, and sent George for the lieutenant. Reynolds hurried to the scene, taking with him Tom Gillespie and Dick Harrison. The lieutenant knocked on the door and told the blacks he was the commander of the rangers and demanded their surrender. They replied with an oath that they would not do so. Reynolds then ordered the house cleared of women and gave the Negroes just five minutes in which to surrender.

Up to this time the women had been quiet, but they now began to scream. This probably demoralized the Negro men. One of them poked McCarthy's pistol, muzzle foremost, out of a window. "Here, come get your damn pistol," he said. McCarthy, a new man in the service, stepped up and grasped it. The instant the Negro felt the touch of McCarthy's hand on the weapon he pulled the trigger. The ball pierced McCarthy's body just above the heart, giving him a mortal wound. At the crack of the pistol the rangers opened fire through the doors and windows on the Negroes within the house. Reynolds and his men then charged the place, and when the smoke of battle cleared they found four dead Negro men and a little Negro girl that had been killed by accident. Only one black escaped. He was hidden under a bed, and as the rangers came in, made a dash to safety under cover of darkness. McCarthy died the following day and was buried near old Fort McKavett. Negro George fought like a tiger and won the boys' praise.[80]

In spite of the foregoing, life at Fort McKavett was rather tame by frontier standards. There was, however, the incident involving the murder of three black troopers by a local rancher named John Monroe "Humpy" Jackson and his accomplices. One of Jackson's colleagues was gunned down in a pasture near Junction City. Neither Jackson nor the remainder of his confederates were ever convicted of the killings by civilian authorities. The incident vexed the post commander for years. (More about "Humpy" follows, in a subsequent chapter.)

Records indicate that the number of troops stationed at Fort McKavett between 1874 and 1875 hovered somewhere between 316 and 443 men. With an average of thirty prisoners locked up in the post jail at any given time, about 10% of the garrison was continually under arrest for one offense or another.[81] In most cases their crimes involved, or grew out of, the excessive consumption of alcohol.

---

[80] Gillett, James B. 1921. *Six Years With The Texas Rangers.* Austin, Texas: Von Boeckmann-Jones Co., Publishers. pp 130-132.
[81] *Fort McKavett Gazette.* Volume 6 Number 1. January 2007.

Troublemakers did not fill out the bulk of the Buffalo Soldier ranks, however. Sergeant Jacob W. Wilks, 9th U.S. Cavalry, is a good example. Jacob W. Wilks was born a slave at Clarke County, Kentucky circa 1840. He escaped, along with his family, via the "Underground Railroad." After his parents died, Wilks was raised in Ohio by the Wadde family. He was among the first men to enlist at Camp Nelson, Kentucky when blacks were first accepted into the military on 16 September 1863. Wilks joined Company "C," 116th Regiment and took part in several Civil War actions, including the defense of Camp Nelson. He served three years and one month. Wilks re-enlisted the same day in Company "F," 9th U S Calvary and was promoted to Sergeant. He served until 1871, and re-enlisted for an additional tour. Wilks was stationed at Fort McKavett from 1869 to 1874, and was in the same Company ("F") as Congressional Medal of Honor winner Emanuel Stance. Wilks eventually contracted chronic lung disease from exposure and was honorably discharged 2 October 1876 from Fort Seldon, New Mexico. He married Elizabeth Moore on 20 October 1884 at Fort McKavett. The couple had six children: Maggie, Mary, Ophelia and Ovelia, Bernice and Mamie Sue. The family moved to San Angelo in 1899 where Wilks purchased land and cattle in Fort McKavett and San Angelo and became successful rancher. He died in 1922 at San Angelo.[82]

Prior to General William Tecumseh Sherman's arrival in Texas the military had not been very aggressive towards hostile Indians. When Sherman hit Texas in the late spring of 1871 it was clear that the earlier policy was about to change. Sherman's inspection tour took him through Fort McKavett on 7 May 1871. Unfortunately his recommendation to President Grant went unheeded until 1874 when Mackenzie's troops were at last loosed against the Indians.

Many of the activities out of Fort McKavett were scouts, conducted by small groups of troopers over short distances which resulted in little or no contact with hostile warriors. One notable exception involved ten troopers of the 9th cavalry under the leadership of Sergeant Emanuel Stance on 20 May 1970. Stance and his men had a chance encounter with Indians near

---

[82] *Fort McKavett Gazette*. Volume 2 Number 2. February 2003.

Kickapoo Creek during which the soldier engaged the Indians three times and captured fourteen horses. For his bravery under fire Sergeant Stance was awarded the Congressional Medal of Honor. Stance was the first black soldier who fought in the Indian War to receive this prestigious honor. (His exploits are covered more thoroughly in a subsequent chapter titled "Buffalo Soldiers.")

Some of the initiatives against hostile Indian tribes that originated at Fort McKavett were wide ranging. During the 1870s Colonel Mackenzie led troops to the upper reaches of the Brazos River, into New Mexico, on a foray against the Kickapoo into Old Mexico, and to the Red River War campaign of 1874.[83]

By 1875, Indian depredations in the area had slowed, although the arrival at Fort McKavett of a German-Texan boy who had been held captive by the Comanches for twelve years was evidence that they had not yet left the plains. By November 1878 companies A, B, and F of the 10th cavalry were ordered back to Fort McKavett from patrol on the Nueces River after having failed to engage in any significant affrays with hostile Indians.[84]

Fort McKavett was finally abandoned. According to local oral histories, the troops began to "lay off the guns" in about 1880. [85] Colonel William R. Shafter arrived on 3 January 1881 to take Command of Fort McKavett.[86] He was the Commander of the 1st U.S. Infantry Regiment and had served at McKavett earlier as Lieutenant Colonel of the 41st and 24th Infantry Regiments.[87] Company D of the 16th Infantry Regiment pulled out in 1883

---

[83] Haley, J. Evetts. 1952. *Fort Concho and the Texas Frontier*. San Angelo, Texas: San Angelo Standard-Times. p 180

[84] *Galveston Daily News*. 30 November 1878.

[85] Hunter, J. Marvin. "Fort McKavett Has Interesting Early History.' *Frontier Times*. Volume 8, Number 2. November 1930. pp 58-60.

[86] Edited by Theophilus Frances Rodenbrough. Bvt. Brigadier General and William L. Haskin. Major, First Artillery. 1896. *The Army of the United States. Historical Sketches of Staff and Line With Portraits of General-in-Chief*. Maynard, Merril & Co. Account of Captain William V. Richards as follows – "In 1880 the regiment was ordered to Texas and was stationed as follows: Headquarters and Company F, first at San Antonio, but soon afterward with D, E, G, H, I and K, at Fort McKavett; A, B, C and I, at Fort Concho."

[87] *Fort McKavett Gazette*. Volume 9 Number 1. January 2010.

and was reassigned to Fort McIntosh on the Rio Grande. Other sources claim that in August 1883 the remaining soldiers were moved to Fort Clark.[88]

The closing of the fort hurt the Fort McKavett community economically, but because residents no longer had to fear for their safety in the absence of troops, they did not scatter as they had when Camp San Saba closed. Not long after the troops left local settlers began to move into the vacated buildings on the post, much as they had done when the military left at the onset of the Civil War.

Post sutler Samuel Wallick remained on site, and operated a general mercantile store. Legitimate businesses from Scabtown moved across the river and joined Wallick on the site of the old post while the less legitimate business vanished one by one. The government decided that the facility would never again be needed, and sold off structures for as little as $50 to $300. Citizens continued to make use of the old fort's structures until the last residents moving out in 1973. By the mid-1890s the community had a doctor, three churches, two hotels, three livery stables, a Masonic lodge, a broom and mattress factory, a weekly newspaper, a stage line with daily service to San Angelo and eighty residents. One enterprising Civil War veteran named William L. Black purchased 30,000 acres west of the old fort and built a canning plant for sheep and goat meat. Unfortunately his business, called the Range Canning Company, was a short-lived venture. Folks were apparently not quite ready for tinned mutton on their grocery shelf. The Fort McKavett school had twenty-eight students and two teachers in 1904. It was later consolidated with the Menard Independent School District.

---

[88] Ibid. p 59.

Courtesy of the *Fort McKavett Gazette*
Volume 7 Number 12. December 2008

By the late 1920s the population of Fort McKavett was estimated at 150. By the 1930s the number had fallen to 136. It remained at that level through the mid 1960s, then dropped to 103 in the 1970s and at forty-five in 1990. Finally, by 2000, there were only fifteen inhabitants.

Fort McKavett had been built to last. Only a fire in 1942 was enough to destroy the commanding officers quarters, which had been constructed in 1854. Efforts to restore the old military post began in the late 1960s, and the site became Fort McKavett Historical Park. Today one may take a leisurely stroll through the grounds of the old fort, which is situated on a picturesque hill near the San Sabá River. There is a wonderful, small museum on the grounds located in the old post hospital building. A number of the original structures have been magnificently restored, allowing the guests to visualize what the fort looked like in its heyday.

William L. Black
Photo courtesy of the Fort McKavett State Historical Site

Range Canning Co. Boiled Mutton
Courtesy of Menardville Museum and Menard Historical Society
Photo from Author's Collection

Post Hospital – Fort McKavett, Texas
Author's Collection

Junior Officers Quarters – Fort McKavett, Texas
Author's Collection

Post Hospital at Fort McKavett – circa 1960
Photo courtesy of the Fort McKavett State Historical Site

Junior Officers Quarters (Lieutenant's Row) – Fort McKavett, Texas
Author's Collection

Post Headquarters – Fort McKavett, Texas
Author's Collection

Fort McKavett circa 1890
Photo Courtesy of Texas Parks and Wildlife

"Scabtown" – Near Fort McKavett
Photo courtesy of the Fort McKavett State Historical Site

Chapter III

John Monroe "Humpy" Jackson

To become a father is not hard, to be a father is, however.
Wilhelm Busch

Some stories are simply too intriguing to overlook. Such is the tale of "Humpy" Jackson, rugged Texas pioneer and proud, protective father.

As is the case in the saga of Billy the Kid, there may be a few factual voids in this yarn considering that it has been passed down over decades. Family genealogists and local historians have been "tweaking" the tale for over a century, in some cases basing aspects on uncorroborated data. None-the-less, "Humpy's" story will help readers grasp the makeup of folks on the Texas frontier.

John Monroe "Humpy" Jackson is believed by most to have been born in Tennessee, circa 1815, although some family genealogists claim Alabama or Georgia as his birthplace. Jackson received the uncomplimentary cognomen of "Humpy" due to the large protuberance on his back. Jackson's first wife, Cynthia Ann Smart, was born circa 1813 at Yell County, Arkansas. The couple had four children - James Monroe (1837-1897) Nancy Jane (1839-1930) David M. (1842-1922) and Rose Ann (1844-1931). Cynthia died after the birth of their daughter Rose Ann at Little Rock, Arkansas.

Jackson second wife was Elizabeth Durham (1822 -1906). They were married in about 1848 at Yell County, Arkansas. By 1854 he had removed to Menard County Texas with his family. The couple had seven children. All but Henrietta were born in Texas:[89]

- Henrietta E. – (1848-1924)

---

[89] Ancestry. Tree #12927330. Person # 55813225.

- Narcissus A. – (1854-1882)
- Martha P. – (1857-1860)
- Sarah Elizabeth "Sallie" – (1861-1954)
- Susan Christine – (1864-1854)
- John Robert – (1868-1954)
- Josie Lenora – (1871-1948)

Jackson is claimed to have built a picket shelter on the original townsite of Menardville, then later relocated east of the town on the San Saba River where the family prospered. Some sources claim that Jackson's homestead was near the old San Saba Mission site.[90]

John Monroe "Humpy" & Elizabeth Durham Jackson circa 1860
Ancestry Files

After the Civil War federal soldiers again occupied the once vacated site of Fort McKavett. Many of the older structures at the compound had suffered from lack of attention over the decades and required major refurbishment. Others had been hastily constructed in the first place, and as a result had

---

[90] Warren, John. "The Vengeance of "Humpy" Jackson." *Frontier Times*. Volume 4 Number 11. August 1927. p 9.

deteriorated rapidly. The fort's commanding officer ordered a sawmill to be erected between Menardville and the Jackson farm to produce the lumber needed for rebuilding the dilapidated buildings. Labor for the lumber mill and shingle operation was provided by the fort's ample supply of Buffalo Soldiers. Details of troopers occupied the mill almost continuously, and frequently drifted into the town of Menardville.

A small local school, attended by fifteen or twenty provincial children, had recently been undertaken near Menardville.[91] According to legend, the Jackson children passed the millworks daily, on their way to and from the newly established school. A Buffalo Soldier sergeant named "Lanky Jim" became infatuated with one of the young Jackson girls. Apparently "Lanky Jim" transferred his heart-felt affections to paper, and had the note delivered to the young Jackson girl. Although one might not immediately deduce it from an examination of the photographic image of "Humpy" and his wife, obviously a "common" pair, the couple are said to have been the progenitors of several of the most attractive young women in the county.

It was not so much the content of "Lanky Jim's" missives that evoked the rage of Jackson but rather the fact that the young romantic was a mulatto sergeant (Seminole Indian scout) in the 9th Cavalry who was stationed at the nearby fort.[92] "Lanky Jim" was apparently either black, of mixed black and Indian blood slaves, or the descendants of slaves who had escaped to Florida to live with the Seminole Indians. Precisely which is unclear.

With perfect innocence and girlish simplicity, Jackson's daughter brought "Lanky Jim's" lover letter home to show her mother. Whether the girl took this action for assistance with ciphering, or to solicit praise for having caught the eye of a fellow, is not known. The letter was apparently overflowing with expressions of Jim's love for the young girl, attesting the he was ready to "…fly away with her in his company."[93] But

---

[91] Warren, John. "The Vengeance of "Humpy" Jackson." *Frontier Times*. Volume 4 Number 11. August 1927. p 9.

[92] Perhaps the fact that "Lanky Jim" was a Seminole scout sergeant explains why no account of his death assigns him a surname.

[93] Warren, John. "The Vengeance of "Humpy" Jackson." *Frontier Times*. Volume 4 Number 11. August 1927. p 9.

Sergeant "Lanky Jim," who is claimed to have spent most of his time loafing at Menardville when not hanging around the sawmill, had unknowingly hit the Trifecta of post-Civil War southern prejudices. He was a Yankee, a trooper, and of mixed Indian and black ancestry. Predictably, trouble soon followed.[94]

Jackson, although a good hearted soul, loyal family man and devilishly hard worker was like many of his Southern contemporaries of the era. He possessed all the prejudices of his ilk. Resting in the shade of a tree near the house "Humpy" heard the text of the letter being red by his wife. He arose in anger, swearing a blood oath against the would-be mulatto paramour.

Jackson was born in the South, and had moved first to Arkansas and then to the San Saba Valley of Texas. He settled at what came to be known as the Five-Mile Crossing, near where Menardville (Menard) is today. Jackson remained in Texas during the Civil War. Like most Texans living on the fringe of civilization, "Humpy" was a veteran of countless hostile encounters with Comanche and Apache Indians who frequented the region, preying on settlers.[95] After the Civil War, like most citizens in the area, he had welcomed the reopening of the fort. Indian depredations had been steadily on the increase while the region went unprotected. The fact that black troops had been stationed at Fort McKavett was not initially viewed with favor by many. Admittedly, the Hill Country region was settled by a variety of European immigrants, some of whom were Union sympathizers. During the Civil War they had voted their anti-slavers position when Texas polled for succession. Needless to say the diversity of views on this matter was the root of many a conflict during the antebellum years, and for decades afterwards.

The fact that Fort McKavett was manned by black soldiers seemed to spoil things for Jackson, who had a reputation as a very stubborn and protective fellow. At the time of the incident with the troopers, Jackson had two teenaged daughters, one named Henrietta and one Narcissus. The girls, who were

---

[94] Ibid. p 9.
[95] Ibid. p 9.

counted among the most beautiful young women in Menard County, had four equally fetching younger sisters and three brothers to round out their clan.

On 9 June 1869 Jackson concealed himself in a stand of tall weeds or undergrowth near the sawmill.[96] When he saw a black soldier who he thought was "Lanky Jim" leaning against a tree taking his evening rest he opened fire. The bullet found its mark, but the target was not "Lanky Jim." Jackson had executed the wrong black man.[97] Or had he?

Jackson's victim was Private Boston Henry. Some sources assert that "Humpy" Jackson intended to kill Henry, claiming that it had been Henry who acted as the romantic messenger and had delivered the love letter on "Lanky Jim's" behalf to Jackson's daughter. Although Boston Henry might have been the courier of the love note, it was Private William Eckles of Company F, 4th Infantry who was actually "Lanky Jim's" penman.[98] Without "Humpy's" own testimony we will probably never know if Boston Henry was his intended target.

Further complicating the matter is the fact that no one actually saw Jackson fire the shot that killed Boston Henry. "Humpy" had been seen in the area before the shooting, toting his squirrel rifle, but that in itself proves nothing with regard to his involvement in Henry's murder.[99] That pesky little detail is confirmed in correspondence between Lieutenant George E. Albee and the acting post adjutant at Fort Concho, thus "Humpy" was charged with the killing based only upon "…the strongest kind of circumstantial evidence."[100]

Sergeant Henry Combs, Company E of the 9th Cavalry, was in charge of the work detail that Private Boston Henry was

---

[96] National Archives and Records Administration (NARA). Washington, D.C.. Letter from First Lieutenant George E. Albee to Second Lieutenant Eugene D. Dimmick, acting post adjutant. Fort Concho, Texas. 1 July 1869.
[97] Hunter, John Warren. "The Vengeance of Humpy Jackson". *Frontier Times Magazine*, Vol. 4, No. 11. August 1927. p 9.
[98] National Archives and Records Administration (NARA). Washington, D.C.. Letter from First Lieutenant George E. Albee to Second Lieutenant Eugene D. Dimmick, acting post adjutant. Fort Concho, Texas. 1 July 1869.
[99] National Archives and Records Administration (NARA). Washington, D.C.. Letter from First Lieutenant George E. Albee to Second Lieutenant Eugene D. Dimmick, acting post adjutant. Fort Concho, Texas. 1 July 1869.
[100] Ibid. p 2.

assigned to on the day of the murder. Combs made no effort to ascertain the identity of Henry's killer nor did he lift a finger to attempt to apprehend the shooter. When questioned later regarding his failure to act his flimsy excuse was that "...he had no orders what to do."[101]

Jackson's detractors, along with a score of revisionist historians bent on underscoring the racial component of the story, are quick to claim that Jackson, in his blind rage, had no specific target in mind and simply shot the first black man he saw. Most, however, believe that "Jackson's" bullet was intended for "Lanky Jim" thus the Henry shooting was a mistake.[102]

Once word of "Humpy's" shooting affray reached the surrounding Hill Country populace it quickly became clear that prevailing sympathies in Menard County lay with Jackson...not with the murder victim. The Army could expect no help from the citizenry. The bitterly fought Civil War had only ended four years earlier with General Robert E. Lee's surrender on 9 April 1865. Reconstruction and "Radical Republican Rule" in Texas wound not be over for another eight years, until after the December 1873 statewide election which resulted in the defeat of widely unpopular Governor Edmund J. Davis by Richard Coke. Returning Confederate soldiers found their families scattered, farmland in ruin and livestock hopelessly dispersed. Jobs were few, and Yankee carpetbaggers controlled local politics. Crime was rampant. Between 1865 and 1868 there were 939 murders committed. Of that total, 460 were by whites against whites, 373 were whites murdering blacks, 10 were blacks killing whites, and 57 were blacks slaying blacks. A later report increased the total number of murders in the period to 1,035. These figures did not include all of Texas, however, since some counties did not file reports.[103]

On 9 June 1869, Lieutenant John L. Bullis ordered the capture of Jackson, who he referred to as "a horse thief and a murderer." Bullis and six troopers combed the area for four

---

[101] Ibid. p 2.
[102] Ibid. p 9.
[103] Johnson, John G. "State Police". Handbook of Texas. Accessed 17 July 2011.

days. Their search covered more than 400 miles. Not surprisingly, locals claimed to have no knowledge of his whereabouts. Jackson, who knew the hills and valleys of the area intimately, was nowhere to be found.

During the following months Jackson regularly slipped back to his house to rest, and to await the next posse of pursuers. When news of a new scout by Bullis' men was passed to him he would once again vanish into the surrounding hills. Some have reported that Jackson made an escape tunnel running from his cellar to the river. Considering the notoriously rocky terrain of the region, that claim may lack veracity. None-the-less, no fewer than a half dozen locals profess to having "Humpy's tunnel" on their ranch.

Jackson managed to maintain his pattern of deception for months, while his pursuers ranged the countryside on a fool's errand. Not unlike the clever rabbit being pursued by the fox, ultimately his luck run out.

According to some accounts, Jackson's daughter Henrietta had made a trip into Menardville where some soldiers from Fort McKavett spotted her and placed her under close scrutiny. When she left town to return home she spurred her horse at top speed to alert her father that the soldiers were in close pursuit. According to First Lieutenant George E. Albee's report of 17 June 1869, he went directly to the to Jackson home that day looking for him "…but failed as his daughter signaled him by firing a revolver in the air."[104] Jackson heard the signal, saw the group approaching and fled, once again making his escape into the hills.

Seven long and embarrassing months passed during which Lieutenant Bullis and the men of the 9th Cavalry were unable to pick up Jackson's trail. Local citizens continued to offer no help. On 1 February 1870, a detail of troopers caught sight of

---

[104] National Archives and Records Administration (NARA). Washington, D.C.. First Lieutenant George E. Albee's report to Captain Gamble at Fort Concho. 17 June 1869. Four months later, on 28 October 1869, Lieutenant George E. Albee was involved in an Indian fight at the Brazos River and was awarded the Congressional Medal of Honor for his bravery in that action. The award was issued on 18 January 1894. The citation reads in part "…Attacked with 2 men a force of 11 Indians, drove them from the hills, and reconnoitered the country beyond."

Jackson and gave chase. During the pursuit Jackson was tossed from his horse by a low hanging branch and took a brutal fall. Convinced that he might be seriously hurt the soldiers took Jackson to his nearby home.

A neighbor, Peter Robertson, had a chance encounter with the captors while heading to Menardville to attend a festival. The troops proudly boasted that three black soldiers were left behind to guard "Humpy," and that he was to be transported to Fort McKavett the following day where he would be locked in the stockade.[105] When Robertson arrived at Menardville he recounted the tale of Jackson's capture to the townspeople. News spread through the tight knit little Hill Country community like a flash flood. Not unexpectedly, neighbors rushed to Jackson's aid. A posse of Jackson supporters mounted up and headed out of town at a gallop.

Back at the Jackson residence, "Humpy" was in bed recovering from the fall. Unbeknownst to the black troopers the old man was not nearly as injured as he had pretended to be. According to some reports, Jackson's wife slipped him a six-gun, which he concealed beneath the bedclothes. Others claim that Jackson's daughter was the one who passed him the pistol, while telling him of a plan hatched by his friends to rescue him. While the troopers guarding him were intentionally distracted, Jackson sprang from his bed with his pistol blazing. Two soldiers, Corporal Albert Marshall and Private Charles Murray, were killed outright.[106] One of the troopers was killed by Jackson. The other was dispatched by one Jackson's friends who had come to his aid…either Charles Owens, Pete Crane, Steve Caviness or George Harvey. The surviving cavalryman, Dan Brown, managed to escape without injury.[107]

Jackson quickly gathered some provisions, commandeered a mount at a neighboring ranch, and escaped. Trooper Brown

---

[105] Hunter, John Warren. "The Vengeance of Humpy Jackson". *Frontier Times Magazine*, Vol. 4, No. 11. August 1927. p 10.
[106] Murray, Charles – Died 2 February 1870 - Pvt. Co F, 9th Cavalry - Lot 890, Block E. Marshall, Albert – Died 2 February 1870 - Corporal Co F, 9th Cavalry - Lot 891, Block E
[107] Hunter, John Warren. "The Vengeance of Humpy Jackson". *Frontier Times Magazine*, Vol. 4, No. 11. August 1927. p 10.

made a dash for Fort McKavett where he reported the bloody incident to Colonel Ranald S. Mackenzie.

The relentless Lieutenant Bullis, accompanied by his scout John DeLong, mounted a new quest. As usual, Jackson managed to elude escape. This time his wife and children were placed under arrest. Although they were jailed for only a brief time, in their absence enraged black troopers burned the Jackson home to the ground in retaliation for the killings of Marshall and Murray.

Knowing that they would be pursued for their role in freeing "Humpy", Pete Crane, Steve Caviness and George Harvey returned to Menardville to procure horses suitable for their flight from the cavalry. Local resident George Kemp fronted the men $75 for the purpose and they made their break.[108]

Some of Jackson's confederates were eventually rounded up and marched in front of trooper Dan Brown for identification, however Brown was unable to recognize any of them as being among the men who were involved in the shooting of Marshall and Murray.

Two weeks hence Colonel MacKenzie somehow managed to obtain the identities of the attackers, no doubt from a whiskey soaked and loose lipped local informant. Their names were out. By 15 February 1870, a sizeable reward had been offered for Stephen Caviness, Peter Crane, George E. Harvey and Charles Owens. William Epps and B.P. Smith were also named, and later arrested as possible accessories.[109]

On 12 April 1870, a choleric Colonel Ranald S. Mackenzie dispatched Captain Carroll, Lieutenant Bullis, John DeLong the guide and nine buffalo soldiers back into the countryside to

---

[108] Hunter, John Warren. "The Vengeance of Humpy Jackson". *Frontier Times Magazine*, Vol. 4, No. 11. August 1927. p 11.

[109] Stephen Caviness was born 28 February 1841, at Benton County, Arkansas. He died 13 April 1870, at Kimble County, Texas.

Caviness never married. It is claimed that he served as a soldier in the Confederate Army, however no documents to verify that service have been uncovered. One source lists service as a Texas Ranger private in Frontier Regiment Company D (or Company E), under Captain N.D. McMillan.[109]

According to local historians, the location of Caviness' killing is on Ranch Road 2291, on the east side near Bear Creek (Viejo Creek) Cemetery, approximately ten and one-tenths miles northwest from the Courthouse in Junction, Texas.

begin yet another reconnoiterer.¹¹⁰ The patrol traveled about twenty miles south by southwest towards Copperas Creek, then to the North Llano River near Moore's Ranch at Cleo where they made camp.

Stephen Caviness
Ancestry Files

At this point in the "Humpy" Jackson saga it may be worth interjecting the fact that Colonel MacKenzie was notoriously over-zealous in his military activities, and was destined to be declared completely insane by the time of his death at age forty nine – nineteen years hence. Obviously the colonel was demonstrating early symptoms of his derangement by 1870.

Bullis, with his patrol of nine soldiers, traveled up Viejo Creek (now Bear Creek) to a pasture belonging to Rance Moore

---

¹¹⁰ National Archives and Records Administration (NARA). Washington, D.C.. Lieutenant Bullis' report to Captain Carroll on the killing of Steven [Stephen] Cavendish [Caviness]. 19 April 1870. Bullis' letter indicates that the scout began on 11 April, not 12 April as is generally cited.

where, at about 10:00 AM on 13 Aril 1870, Stephen Caviness was finally located. The intrepid Caviness fled, and managed to escape capture. At about 4:00 PM Bullis, the guide and eight troops gave chase for about ten miles. They were unable to locate Caviness.

At about 11:00 AM on the 14th Lieutenant Bullis and his men finally caught up with Caviness. In a report that followed, Bullis claimed that they shot and killed Caviness "only after he resisted their arrest efforts."[111] Local Hill Country folks gave little credence to Bullis' story then, nor do their descendants believe it now.

Caviness is buried in the Bear Creek Cemetery at Cleo in Kimble County, which was at one time part of the Moore pasture. His grave is marked by a rock fence enclosure.[112] Lieutenant Bullis and his men took Caviness' horse, saddle, spurs and guns back to Captain Carroll, presumably as trophies or bona-fides of the kill.[113]

Stephen "Steve" Caviness hailed from the town of Streeter, which is located between Big and Little Bluff creeks, southeast of Menardville and nine miles west of Mason in neighboring Mason County. Around 1855 Irish settlers, including William S. "Uncle Billy" Gamel and the Caviness brothers moved to the area. Not long after German settlers followed, and a small community began to take shape. The earliest families located along Big and Little Bluff creeks and nearby Honey Creek, so the community was called both the Bluff Creek or Honey Creek Community. As was the case with Menard County, early settlers suffered mightily from Indian raids. Dean Martin and Tom

---

[111] National Archives and Records Administration (NARA). Washington, D.C.. Lieutenant Bullis' report to Captain Carroll on the killing of Steven [Stephen] Cavendish [Caviness].

[112] Bear Creek Cemetery grew up around the gravesite of Caviness. The second person to be buried there was James Sewell, who had brought his young bride to Cleo from Coleman County in 1868. At about eleven o'clock a party of Indians, about fifty in number, passed though the county and found James Sewell making rails. They killed him, scalped him, took his horse and moved on down the country about five miles where they killed three cows and one yearling and were feasting on them when they were trailed and attacked by nine citizens.

[113] Wyatt, Frederica Burt. "A Bad Time in Kimble County". *The Junction Eagle, Hunters & Visitors Guide 2002*. Wednesday, 30 October 2002. pp 38-39

Brite opened the first stores at Streeter. Charles Brite operated a gin and flourmill there as well. The community selected the name Streeter when a post office was applied for and established on 5 September 1890. According to tradition, the first postmaster, Joseph A. Black, selected the name in honor of an early settler named Samuel T. Streeter. By about 1925 the population had dropped to 100, where it remains today.[114] From all accounts, Stephen Caviness was an outgoing individual, and had many friends in the area. Caviness was among the scouts who engaged in an Indian fight on 2 April 1862 at nearby Saline, in Menard County. The incident is believed to have stemmed from the tragic massacre of Henry and Nancy Dorsey Parks and their grandson at Saline.

Eventually "Humpy" Jackson's other cohorts drifted away from the region, but not before several men of the community had been arrested for suspicion of having helped in his escape. In the end, none were officially charged. William Epps and B.P. Smith were held in the guardhouse at Fort McKavett in February 1870 for a time, but there was insufficient evidence to proceed against them.[115] In a clear display of the extent of overreaching and abuse of power MacKenzie was capable of, "Humpy's" wife Elizabeth along with their daughter Henrietta were also incarcerated in MacKenzie's stockade, under suspicion of having had a hand in the killing of Corporal Marshall. They too were soon released.[116] About all that MacKenzie had accomplished during his medieval style inquest was to further alienate the local populace and execute a respected Indian fighter, war hero and local citizen...Stephen Caviness.

Troopers continued their quest for "Humpy" Jackson for about two more years. In spite of their diligent efforts Jackson,

---

[114] Alice J. Rhoades, "STREETER, TX," *Handbook of Texas*. Also see - Eilers, Kathryn Burford. 1939. *A History of Mason County, Texas*. M.A. thesis. University of Texas. Hunter, J. Marvin. "Brief History of Mason County." *Frontier Times*. November, December 1928.

[115] National Archives and Records Administration (NARA). Washington, D.C.. Letter of Colonel Ranald S. Mackenzie to Colonel H. Clay Wood. 15 February 1870.

[116] Ibid.

who continued to be aided by family and loyal friends, was never again apprehended.

"Humpy" Jackson eventually surrendered on his own. On 14 June 1871, he appeared in Menardville and posted his $2,000 bond. According to Menardville citizen Mrs. A.W. Noguess, Jackson's decision to turn himself in took place only after "our country got out from under martial law...and we were allowed to have courts."[117]

A civilian court eventually tried Jackson at the nearby town of Mason. All charges against him were dismissed, and "Humpy" Jackson returned home.

Contemporary historians will rush to point out that a terrible injustice was done by an obviously prejudiced jury when they freed Jackson, and that he had gotten away Scott free with the murder of at least two black men who were troopers in the United States Army. Few, however, will mention the fact that no one saw Jackson fire the shot that killed Boston Henry, and that there was no physical evidence of any kind. Charges were brought based on the fact that he had been seen in the area carrying his squirrel rifle. As cited earlier, the highly respected Lieutenant George E. Albee, soon to be a Congressional Medal of Honor recipient, pointed out that "Humpy" was charged with the killing based on only "...the strongest kind of circumstantial evidence."[118] Trooper Dan Brown was unable to positively identify Jackson, or for that matter any of his colleagues, as the shooter in the Marshall and Murray killings.

None-the-less, based on oral histories and legend, most are inclined to agree that "Humpy" was probably guilty of the killing of Boston Henry. As to the identity of the person or persons that fatally shot Corporal Albert Marshall and Private Charles Murray, "Humpy's" role in that incident is cloudy as well. Once again, most believe that "Humpy" was responsible for at least the Marshall shooting. However, the fact that Colonel MacKenzie held Jackson's wife Elizabeth along with their daughter Henrietta in custody under suspicion of being the killers should be proof enough that there was insufficient

---

[117] Weider History Group. Copyright 1999 Gale, Cengage Learning.
[118] Ibid. p 2.

evidence to prove the identity of the person or persons who actually did the deed.

More than six years had passed since the shooting of Private Boston Henry. Three black soldiers, as well as Jackson's confederate Stephen Caviness, lay dead. All this over a love note.

Written accounts of the "Lanky Jim" incident refer to Jackson as an "a very old man" at the time, although he was probably only fifty-five at the time.[119] Physically diminished from the rigors of being on the run for an extended time, Jackson was no longer as robust a man as he had been. He remained in the area. Jackson was never again as financially secure as he had been before the "Lanky Jim" ordeal. The army had taken all of his livestock, terrorized his family and burned his home to the ground. He did manage to build another house to replace the one that had been torched by the angry black troopers. He also managed to father another daughter.

John Monroe "Humpy" Jackson died on 23 December 1890. He is buried at the Pioneer Rest Cemetery in Menard. Elizabeth Durham-Jackson died circa 1906. Although as yet unverified, some family genealogists report the date as 27 February 1905.

The "Humpy" Jackson legend lives on. During the period that he is said to have been aggressively pursued by MacKenzie's forces storytellers claim that "Humpy" concealed himself in the brush on one of the many peaks overlooking the Menardville/Fort McKavett road waiting for a black cavalrymen to pass. When he spotted his prey "Humpy's" long range rifle would erupt and another black soldier would bite the dust. The remains of these soldiers are said to have been carted to the graveyard at Fort McKavett, or buried along the winding trail.[120] Although this tale makes for exciting reading, its veracity is keenly dubious.

In spite of the fact that there are records of at least nineteen soldiers who died between 1869 and 1871 who were interred at

---

[119] National Archives and Records Administration (NARA). Washington, D.C.. First Lieutenant George E. Albee's report to Captain Gamble at Fort Concho. 17 June 1869.

[120] Hunter, John Warren. "The Vengeance of Humpy Jackson". *Frontier Times Magazine*, Vol. 4, No. 11. August 1927. p 12.

the Fort McKavett Cemetery (most later moved to the National Cemetery at San Antonio) it is impossible to verify the truthfulness of this aspect of the "Humpy" yarn.[121]

"Humpy" Jackson's story has been retold by each successive generation for nearly 150 years. One may fault Old "Humpy" for his racial bias, but not for his determination and his resolute defense of his family on the rugged Texas frontier.

Grave of John Monroe "Humpy" Jackson
Pioneer Rest Cemetery – Menard, Texas
Photo from Author's Collections

---

[121] Records of the Fort McKavett Cemetery. Menard County, Texas. Compiled by Frederica Burt Wyatt. Submitted by Gloria B. Mayfield. Assisted by Coordinator, Dolores I. Bishop. 6 July 2000. Also – Ground penetrating radar equipment was used to survey the Fort McKavett cemetery site. The survey discovered that although the tombstones of many of the soldiers who had been interred there may have been moved to the National Cemetery at San Antonio, it appears as though the bodies of the men were not.

Grave of Stephen Caviness
Bear Creek Cemetery – Cleo, Texas
Photo from Author's Collections

Original Tombstone of Stephen Caviness
Bear Creek Cemetery – Cleo, Texas
Photo from Author's Collections

Chapter IV

John Wesley Vaden

> *The evil that men do lives after them;*
> *The good is oft interred with their bones.*
> **William Shakespeare**

Practically every Texas town boasts having at least one lawman from the "Old West" era who was gunned down on the streets, or in one of the saloons, of their fine community. Fort McKavett in Menard County is no exception. Deputy Sheriff John Wesley Vaden holds the distinction of being the only lawman to meet such a fate during the 1800s. Although perhaps not the community's finest example of a model citizen, Vaden was none-the-less a legitimately appointed lawman at the time of his death.

Information about John W. Vaden has proven to be somewhat contentious. Account of his misdeeds by family genealogists occasionally runs afoul of period accounts, and of those done by reliable historians.[122] According to limited records, and family genealogists, Vaden was born in Alabama on 22 February 1849, to Amos Garrett and Mary Ann (Wallace) Vaden.[123] His parents had come from Tennessee.[124] John Vaden was the eldest of the couple's eleven children. We also know that he was gunned down on 7 October 1886 at Fort McKavett. Some claim that his death was nothing short of a cold-blooded murder. Others maintain that his killer acted in self-defense.[125]

---

[122] Page, Anita Vaden. 1997. *Badges, Bullets and Blood: The Murder of John Vaden by Ben Daniels*. Silver City, New Mexico.
[123] Ancestry. Tree 27102814. Person 12116169400.
[124] Ibid.
[125] Page. *Badges, Bullets and Blood: The Murder of John Vaden by Ben Daniels*.

Apart from the gaps and sparse record of his mortal journey we do know that, according to all reliable accounts, Vaden was an undisputedly acrimonious character who became contemptible when drunk.[126] Regrettably, it seems he was often intoxicated, and is said to have been "a reckless and dangerous man when he was drinking."[127] As one respected author recently declared, "If ever a man needed killing, John W. Vaden qualified."[128]

Based on practically all written accounts of John Vaden it seems that any attempt to portray him as having been anything other than an ignominious good-for-nothing and an incessant boozer would be fruitless and factually dishonest. None-the-less, the treatise written by a family descendent does assert otherwise.[129]

Precisely how, and when, Vaden wound up in Texas is unclear. For some reason Texas seemed to have collected an astounding array of nefarious, profligate rascals during the post-Civil War reconstruction era. Vaden is claimed to have ridden with the much-maligned Ben Bickerstaff and his gang of derelicts and malefactors.[130] Vaden gunned down three black men and cut off their ears as keepsakes, presumably in revenge for the ambush and murder of his step-uncle Gabriel Jackson.[131] He carried his trophies in a pouch with a drawstring, and proudly displayed whenever implored to do so.[132] Not long after the Civil War had ended he is credited with killing three Union soldiers along with the black man they were guarding.

---

[126] Alexander, Bob. 2007. *Lawmen, Outlaws and S.O.B.'s, Volume II: Gunfigthers of the Old West*. Silver City, New Mexico: High-Lonesome Books.
[127] Loomis, John A. 1982. *Texas Ranchman*. Chardon, Nebraska: The Fur Press. p 13.
[128] DeArment, Bob. "The Killing of John W. Vaden by a Man Named Ben Daniels," *Wild West History Journal*. Volume 1. Number 1. February 2008. p 5.
[128] Page. *Badges, Bullets and Blood: The Murder of John Vaden by Ben Daniels*. Silver. p 5.
[129] Ibid.
[130] Alexander. *Lawmen, Outlaws and S.O.B.'s, Volume II: Gunfigthers of the Old West*.
[131] Page. *Badges, Bullets and Blood: The Murder of John Vaden by Ben Daniels*. Silver. p 6.
[132] Ibid. p 168.

Bickerstaff, who was born in Mississippi in 1839, had served in Co. H, 11th Texas Cavalry during the Civil War.[133] Gangs led by such outlaws as Cullen M. Baker, Benjamin F. Bickerstaff, and Bob Lee preyed on the people of northeastern Texas. Their targets were often freedmen or federal soldiers. This collection of ruthless murderers and horse thieves could hardly be called political activists.

On 18 October 1868 Lieutenant Gustavus Schreyer, along with three corporals and fifteen privates were sent in pursuit of the outlaw Ben Bickerstaff. They succeeded in capturing prisoners and also a quantity of horses and arms.[134] They did not, however, get Bickerstaff. Ultimately his misdeeds caught up with him. Citizens of the town of Alvarado shot him down in the street just as he and his compatriot Josiah Thompson arrived and were dismounting. A barrage of gunfire let loose by enraged townspeople cut Thompson down in his footsteps. He was dead when he hit the ground. Bickerstaff was hit three times, once in the eye.[135] Although he was able to return fire he died shortly after. Both Bickerstaff and Thompson are buried at the Balch Cemetery at Alvarado.

After the style of a true Bickerstaff Gang ne're-do-well, John Vaden is also responsible for the murder of a former Union sympathizer named Lige Reynolds. That incident took place on 29 August 1868 at Sulphur Springs.[136] Reynolds had the misfortune of standing in the door of a barbershop when Vaden rode past on horseback, recognized him, and gunned him down in cold blood.

In 1876 Vaden married Cynthia Louise "Lucy" Matilda (Matelda) Jackson at Menard. "Lucy", a mere child at the time, was the granddaughter of John Monroe "Humpy" Jackson and was only thirteen when she wed Vaden.[137] He was twenty-

---

[133] National Park Service. Civil War Soliders and Sailors System. Bickerstaff, B.F. Microfilm M227 Roll 3.
[134] Muster Roll. Co. H. 6th US Cavalry. 31st day of August 1866 to 31st day of October 1868. US National Archives.
[135] *Galveston Daily News.* 13 April 1869.
[136] DeArment, Bob. "The Killing of John W. Vaden by a Man Named Ben Daniels," *Wild West History Journal.* Volume 1. Number 1. February 2008. p 5.
[137] Page. *Badges, Bullets and Blood: The Murder of John Vaden by Ben Daniels.* Silver. p 6-7. See chapter on "Humpy" Jackson for background on this

seven. Cynthia was the eldest daughter of four, and second oldest of the eight offspring of James Monroe and Emily Ann (Miller) Jackson who had come to Texas from Yell County, Arkansas.

Given the details of his sordid background, it comes as some surprise to know that Vaden enlisted in Captain Dan Roberts' Company D of the Texas Ranger Frontier Battalion on 1 June 1877 and was accepted. He served under Second Lieutenant F. M. Moore who boasts an unblemished record, before and after his Ranger service.[138] Vaden was released in 31 August 1877 after logging only four months of service to the Lone Star State. According to family historians he was shot in the chest by a prisoner while serving as a ranger. The bullet struck a pouch of tobacco in his pocket and lodged there, thus inflicting no real damage to Vaden's person.[139] His official record indicates that he was "honorably discharged."[140] Vaden's detractors are oftentimes hasty in their attempt to insert some hint or speculation of wrongdoing connected with respect to his discharge. Historians, on the other hand, rely on the written records for their facts, and form their hypotheses of Vaden based on the sum total of his story.

At the time of Vaden's ranger service Company D's senior officer, Major John B. Jones, had just completed a major drive during which he rounded up numerous outlaws in neighboring Kimble County. On news of trouble, Jones committed to dispatch three companies of rangers to Junction City by 15 April 1877, with Lieutenant Moore charged with establishing a camp at Bear Creek.[141] Rangers made forty-one arrests during

---

individual.
[138] Moore commanded Company D from September 1876 to September 1877. Partial list of Texas Ranger Company Commanders. Compiled by Christina Stopka. Director, Texas Ranger Research Center.
[139] DeArment, Bob. "The Killing of John W. Vaden by a Man Named Ben Daniels," *Wild West History Journal.* Volume 1. Number 1. February 2008. p 5.
[140] Texas State Library & Archives Commission. Texas Ranger Frontier Battalion Service Records. Call Number 401-175.
[141] Junction was founded in the spring of 1876 following the organization of the county in January of that year. It was originally named Denman after its surveyor, but became Junction City in 1877 and simply Junction in 1894.

their campaign, thirty-seven of which were made in Kimble County.

By 6 May 1877, Major Jones had moved his rangers twenty-five miles north to Fort McKavett. To be certain, the period during which Vaden served as a ranger in the summer of 1877 was a time of relative calm for the Frontier Battalion. It is entirely possible that Vaden saw no action whatsoever during his tenure.[142]

Vaden served as a deputy sheriff in Maverick County. While running for office in Menard County he swaggered about with a Winchester rifle threatening to kill any Mexican who didn't vote for him. Before the polls closed he is said to have kicked out a window of the courthouse where the election was being held because the votes were not being cast as he thought they should be.[143] The very same Vaden who had recklessly disturbed the earlier balloting was elected a justice of the peace for Menard County in 1879. Not long after the Menard County appointment he wound up in jail at Glenrose in early 1880 on a charge of aggravated assault.[144] Charges against him were dismissed due to a legal error by the county attorney. Vaden and his family appear on the census for Somervell for 1880, which was taken on 13 June.[145]

To further round out the reader's image of Vaden, in *Lawmen, Outlaws and S.O.B.'s,* author Bob Alexander wrote that Vaden was "Frequently decried for his wretchedly foul behavior..." and that he "...wasn't bashful about picking on weaklings when it sadistically suited his nasty temperament."

In 1882 ranchman John A. Loomis gave Vaden and his wife both jobs, working on his Silver Cliff sheep ranch near Paint Rock in Concho County. Vaden tended to the flocks of sheep while Lucy served as a cook. Loomis offered no complaint

---

[142] Webb, Walter Prescott. 2003. *The Texas Rangers, A Century of Frontier Defense.* Austin, Texas: University of Texas Press. pp 338-339.
[143] Ibid. p 168. Also see Hunter, John Warren. "Killing of John Vaden at Ft. McKavett." *San Angelo Standard.* 12 October 1912.
[144] Page. *Badges, Bullets and Blood: The Murder of John Vaden by Ben Daniels.* Silver. p 10.
[145] US Census. Census Year 1880. Census Place Precinct 2, Somervell, Texas. Roll 1327. Family History Film 1255327. Page 361D. Enumeration District 147.

regarding Vaden's work, but Lucy's cooking was another matter.[146] "Our menu would not have been bad if Mrs. Vadon [sic] had known just a little about ordinary cooking. She served bacon half fried floating in grease, and the biscuits were almost inedible."[147]

Vaden decided to open a saloon at Ballinger in Runnels County in the summer of 1886.[148] Tom Hill, the former City Marshal of Abilene, had taken the City Marshal's job at Ballinger and left his wife Mollie, two year old daughter Belle and infant son Harry in neighboring Abilene, Taylor County.

Tom Hill was no pantywaist, and his confrontation with Vaden was not a Friday night waltz with a dotard. Hill was born in Kentucky. He joined the army on 2 March 1876, and was sent directly to Fort Fetterman in Wyoming Territory. Those familiar with Wyoming know that Fort Fetterman was centrally located to much of the Indian fighting in that Territory. Hill was involved in his share, feeling the sting of battle and the exhilaration of mortal combat. By all accounts he performed valiantly. Hill was later assigned to Fort Robinson in Nebraska, in the midst of the Sioux Indian uproar, where once again he proved his mettle.

In October 1872, while still a soldier, Hill's family moved from Kentucky to Texas. They first settled near Pilot Point in Denton County, then later removed to Callahan County. Tom Hill rejoined them there after his discharge and pinned on a deputy sheriff's badge.

Hill migrated to nearby Buffalo Gap in Taylor County where he again served as a sheriff's deputy.[149] Buffalo Gap was a double tough, rugged cow town packed with saloons, dance halls and sporting houses and populated with all manner of degenerate, gambler, card sharp, pimp and soiled dove imaginable. Hill eventually moved to nearby Abilene, a burgeoning cow town on the route of the newly built Texas & Pacific Railroad. Abilene had sprung from the Texas soil as a

---

[146] Loomis. *Texas Ranchman*. p 13-14.
[147] Ibid. p 14.
[148] DeArment, Bob. "The Killing of John W. Vaden by a Man Named Ben Daniels." *Wild West History Journal*. Volume 1. Number 1. February 2008. p 7.
[149] Alexander. *Lawmen, Outlaws and S.O.B.'s, Volume II: Gunfigthers of the Old West*. pp 156-169.

rugged and nasty tent city, and like Buffalo Gap was populated with every form of ne'er-do-well imaginable. Over time the town grew to a level of sophistication not exceeded by many frontier Texas cities. At Abilene Hill was both feared and respected as city marshal.

It was at Abilene that Hill met and married Mollie J. Houser, an attractive lass from a well to do Waco family. Hill improved his stature as well as his finances while in Abilene, but soon fell in bad company.

**Gravesite of Texas Ranger Lieutenant F.M. Moore
At Center Point, Texas**
Author's Collection

Hill met a fellow named Jim Holland. After some measure of scheming he and Holland made a fateful trip to New York City where they planned on exchanging $500 in legitimate specie for $10,000 in counterfeit currency. The trip turned out to be a disaster for the pair. An unfortunate encounter with two brothers named Tom and Theodore Davis, who by all accounts were planning on robbing them, resulted in Holland pulling his Colt six-shooter and plugging Tom Davis three times. The outcome was predictable...Davis died ...Hill and Holland wound up in jail. After a bizarre and protracted trial at the hands of condescending "Yankees," Hill managed to get shed of New York and gleefully returned to Texas.[150]

Whether Hill was booted out of Abilene because of his New York escapade remains a matter of conjecture, but he was soon unemployed and the town was looking for a new police chief. Hill had signed on as city marshal in nearby Ballinger.

On 6 August 1886, John Vaden was, once again, intoxicated. He had armed himself with a Winchester rifle and had shot out the lamps in his own establishment. Had he isolated his gunplay to foolishly extinguishing the illumination at his own business the incident would have been no more noteworthy than that of countless other trigger happy drunks who mysteriously felt compelled to take target practice on streetlights, knotholes and billboards. Unfortunately Vaden, packing his Winchester, went to the neighboring Palace Saloon and began creating a disturbance there. The Palace bartender, Frank Bornan, was having none of Vaden's gunplay. The two men tangled, resulting in little more than bloodied noses and blackened eyes.[151] When City Marshal Hill stepped in and attempted to separate the two pugilists Vaden fired his rifle, accidentally hitting Hill in the left foot. As one might expect, the wound was serious. Hill's foot had to be amputated. As author Bob DeArment writes in his article *The Killing of John W. Vaden by a Man Named Ben Daniels* "…the surgery was successful but the patient died." Hill died at 6:00 a.m. on 8 August 1886, reportedly "…from lockjaw or an overdose of chloroform or other causes."[152] Apart from the fact that Hill's death certificate lacked modern day specificity, he was quite dead none-the-less.

Later, the incident reports varied as to the precise circumstances of the shooting. Hill's petty detractors, of whom there were many in his post Abilene days, opined that Hill had actually shot himself in the foot by accident. Others credited Hill with trying to disarm a friend who was slobbering drunk and who was about to get himself into serious trouble. Most

---

[150] Ibid.
[151] *The Fort Worth Gazette.* 7 August 1886.
[152] Alexander. *Outlaws and S.O.B.'s, Volume II: Gunfigthers of the Old West.* p 170.

placed the blame squarely on the shoulders of the drunken John Vaden, however.

Vaden moved back to Menard County, this time to Fort McKavett. Considering that Menard County had just five towns, and Vaden may have worn his welcome thin during his earlier stay at Menardville, Fort McKavett seemed a wise choice when faced with the alternative…the tiny communities of Callan, Saline or Maringo (Hext).[153]

The once disgraced former justice of the peace John Vaden next obtained a commission as a deputy in Menard County under Sheriff J.W. Mears. Not to imply that one cannot shake the evils of the demon rum and go straight, but on 7 October 1886 Vaden went to Mayer's saloon and in due course was, somewhat predictably, intoxicated. Vaden began smashing furniture and creating a disturbance. He picked up a billiard ball and threw it at Benjamin Franklin "Ben" Daniels, barely missing him. Daniels, a bartender who coincidentally was also commissioned in Menard County as a deputy sheriff, closed the saloon, strapped on his pistol and retreated to an old coral at the rear of Mayer's store where he hid out until about 3:00 AM.[154],[155] Next Vaden armed himself with a pike and began terrorizing townspeople, waving and thrusting the pointed spear-like implement of war wildly about at a Mexican patron of Wallick's store until Sam Wallick and others intervened.

Having no human quarry to impale with his pike, Vaden began tormenting a team of hitched horses, lacerating the animals just to see them jump and kick.[156] When Daniels arrived at the scene he suddenly found himself facing Vaden at a distance of twenty feet. Vaden rushed towards him with the

---

[153] Dating to as early as 1757 when the community was a Spanish settlement Menardville was founded in 1858. In 1910 or 1911, while the Fort Worth and Rio Grande Railroad Company was making plans to lay track through the community, company officials asked residents to rename their town Menard in order to facilitate the painting of signs.

[154] Daniels was appointed a "constable or deputy" on 9 June 1885. See - Page, Anita Vaden. 1997. *Badges, Bullets and Blood: The Murder of John Vaden by Ben Daniels*. Silver City, New Mexico. p 15.

[155] Hunter, John Warren. "Killing of John Vaden at Ft. McKavett." *San Angelo Standard*. 12 October 1912. p 18.

[156] Ibid.

long pike. The advance dumbfounded Daniels. He and Vaden had been friends. Daniels had dined at the Vaden home just the previous evening.[157] Daniels commanded him to stop. Weighing his regard for Vaden, and faced with being skewered at his hand, Daniels wisely opened fire. Five shots rang out, four went wild but the fifth struck Vaden in the collarbone and inflicted the soon to be fatal wound. According to the *San Angelo Standard Times* account of the incident, "Vaden walked about twenty yards and fell dead, [saying] 'Daniels, I would not have done you this way for anything.' Daniels mounted his horse and rode off."[158]

Some stories of the incident vary, one claiming that when Vaden thrust the long metal tipped wooden pole at Daniels he stepped aside, drew his pistol and shot the aggressor twice...with one of the bullets passing through Vaden's side. Daniels, according to this account, "borrowed" a horse that was tied up outside and fled, apparently fearing revenge from Vaden's family or friends.[159] A grand jury decided not to prosecute Daniels for the murder.

As cited earlier, there were mixed feelings about the legitimacy of his claim of self-defense. Family genealogists boldly assert that he was "...shot in cold blood while unarmed..." as is inscribed for eternity on his tombstone.[160] They go on to state that "John Vaden may have had his faults, [but] he was not the desperado he has previously been made out to be."[161] Most, however, seem to recount the Daniels incident as just another one of Vaden's ill-fated whiskey fueled rants gone fatally wrong.

John Wesley Vaden was survived by his Cynthia Louise (Lucy) Matilda Jackson and the couple's three children. He is buried at the Fort McKavett Cemetery. The spelling of his surname is sometimes listed as "Varden."[162] Vaden's funeral

---

[157] Ibid.
[158] *San Angelo Standard Times.* 8 October 1886.
[159] DeArment, Bob. "The Killing of John W. Vaden by a Man Named Ben Daniels." *Wild West History Journal.* Volume 1. Number 1. February 2008. p 7.
[160] Page. *Badges, Bullets and Blood: The Murder of John Vaden by Ben Daniels.* p 9.
[161] Page. *Badges, Bullets and Blood: The Murder of John Vaden by Ben Daniels.* p 23.
[162] *Dallas Morning News.* 27 February 1886
    Dallas Morning News. 2 March 1886
    Dallas Morning News. 4 March 1886

was not well attended. "Besides his wife and two or three bright little children there were few mourners".[163]

For over a century scores or historians and authors have contended that the Benjamin Franklin "Ben" Daniels who shot and killed John Vaden Daniels later made quite a reputation for himself as a gunfighter, rode with Teddy Roosevelt as a Rough Rider during the Spanish American War, and eventually became United States Marshal for the Arizona Territory. As author Bob DeArment points out in his article about the Vaden killing, "writers have leaped to the conclusion that the Ben Daniels who snuffed out John Vaden's lights was the same Ben Daniels who rose from gunfighter notoriety to become a presidential favorite and law enforcement officer of high stature."[164]

As it turns out the Ben Daniels who shot and killed Vaden returned the horse he had "borrowed" within a week, as he had promised when he appropriated the animal to facilitate his escape. Daniels remained at Menard County. He later accepted another appointment as deputy sheriff in April 1887, under the new sheriff, R.R. Russell. At precisely the same time as Vaden's killer Ben Daniels was in Menard County, the "other Ben Daniels" who would eventually rise to fame as a lawman was running a saloon, gambling den and dance hall at Dodge City, Kansas and was under a $10,000 bail for the murder of a man named Ed Julian in that same town.[165] Clearly the fellow from Dodge City, Kansas with the surname of Daniels was not the same fellow who killed Vaden.

The Ben Daniels who killed Vaden seems to have disappeared from Menard County, and history, after serving out his April 1887 term as deputy.

Fort Worth Gazette. 7 August 1886
Dallas Morning News. 9 August 1886
Austin Daily Statesman. 13 August 1886
Dallas Morning News. 15 September 1886

[163] Hunter, John Warren. "Killing of John Vaden at Ft. McKavett." *San Angelo Standard.* 12 October 1912. p 18.
[164] DeArment, Bob. "The Killing of John W. Vaden by a Man Named Ben Daniels." *Wild West History Journal.* Volume 1. Number 1. February 2008. p 9.
[165] Ibid. p 11.

Tombstone of John Vaden – Fort McKavett, Texas
Photo from Author's Collection

Chapter V

Silver & The Lost Bowie Mine
La Mina de las Almagres

> *What is life but a series of inspired follies?*
> *The difficulty is to find them to do.*
> **George Bernard Shaw**

Perhaps more gripping to the adventure seeker than the stories of long forgotten communities like Hext, Callan and Saline is the saga of the search for silver in the Texas hills, and the legendary Lost Bowie Mine. It has been a topic of conversation, controversy, and speculation for well over a century and a half.

Did the Spanish really mine silver and gold in Texas during the 1700's or, as some have alleged, did they use exploratory shafts to store silver bars mined somewhere else? Did James and Rezin Bowie actually search for this legendary mine?

Where to begin, and end, this story is a dilemma. One early work on the topic claimed that "Unexacting Indians who gathered at the mission [Mission Santa Cruz de San Sabá] to be instructed in the worship of the Christian God suddenly found themselves enslaved and forced into the mine tunnels to dig silver day and night."[166] This source goes on to claim that "Finally the Indians revolted, killing every priest, soldier and Spaniard at the mine, church and fort."[167] Of course, we know from correspondence of the day that the foregoing is not completely accurate. Not all were killed. None-the-less, literally volumes of data have been written about the Lost Bowie Mine, more properly known by serious historians and researchers as La Mina de las Almagres, La Mina de las Iguanas, the Los

---

[166] Eckhardt, C.F. 1982. *The Lost San Sabá Mines.* Austin, Texas: Texas Monthly Press. p 11.
[167] Ibid. p 12.

Almagres Mine, or Lost San Sabá Mine. Offering a concise summary seems to be the most appropriate path so far as this treatise is concerned. Perhaps by so doing the interested reader may be bitten by the treasure hunting bug and join the century and a half long quest for hidden silver in the Texas Hill Country.

Charlie F. Eckhardt, of Seguin, Texas, spent years researching his book *The Lost San Saba Mines*. Those who follow this topic seem to agree that it is one of the best ever written on this subject-matter. In 1991, *Treasure Magazine* published a six-part article about the mine and the legend that is said to be equally telling.

According to reliable sources, an expedition in 1753 seeking a site for an Apache mission eventually led to the discovery of the Los Almagres Mine in what is now Llano County.[168] Some sources establish the year as 1752.[169] Lieutenant Juan Galván heard about a hill of red ocher indicating the presence of mineral-bearing ores from local Indians. In August 1753 several men from that settlement were guided to the site by Apache Indians. No valuable ore was found. Governor Jacinto de Barrios y Jáuregui, who was concerned that using Apache guides might arouse the ire of the Comanches, sent an official expedition led by the wealthy, high bred officer and member of the *hidalgo* class named Bernardo de Miranda y Flores.[170] Miranda y Flores left San Antonio with twenty-three people - sixteen soldiers, five citizens and two interpreters on 17 February 1756. In his journal Miranda y Flores describes the journey and their findings, claiming that "...I guarantee to give a mine to each one of the inhabitants of the province of Texas..."[171]

---

[168] Weddle, Robert S. Weddle. 1964. *The San Sabá Mission*. Austin, Texas: University of Texas Press

[169] Desmond, H.A. 1976. *My Search for Las Almagres Mine, Later Called Bowie's Mine*. Bi-Centenial Edition 1976. Pages not numbered.

[170] A *hidalgo* is a member of the Spanish and Portuguese nobility. In popular usage it has come to mean the non-titled nobility. *Hidalgos* were exempt from paying taxes, but did not necessarily own real property. The feminine is *hidalga* in Spanish and *fidalga*. See - Mackay, Angus .1977. *Spain in the Middle Ages: From Frontier to Empire, 1000-1500*. New York, New York: St. Martin's Press.

The site of Mission Santa Cruz de San Sabá, supposedly near the mine site, is located on present day FM 2092, about three miles east of Menard. Colonel Diego Ortiz Parrilla arrived at that location on 17 April 1757. Ortiz Parrilla spent five days picking a spot, which he eventually laid out on the north side of the San Saba River. The Presidio San Luis de las Amarillas site was located about 4½ miles to the west.

After locating a region now known as the Riley Mountains near Honey Creek, Miranda's men discovered "a tremendous stratum of ore."[172]. So abundant were the ore veins, Miranda boldly guaranteed "a mine to each of the inhabitants of the province of Texas." They named the mine San José del Alcazar.

Following Miranda's return to San Antonio on 10 March 1756, Barrios sent a three-pound ore sample to the viceroy's agent in Mexico City, Manuel de Aldaco (Albaco), for assay. The sample was deemed too small for accurate analysis. Aldaco suggested that thirty mule-loads of the material be sent for further testing. For a variety of reasons that never happened. Some have claimed that Aldaco's report was intentionally skewed, musing that if Miranda had actually discovered a successful mine the viceroy might cut him out in favor of Miranda.[173]

In the meantime, the Apache mission and a presidio were established on the San Sabá River near the site of present-day Menard. The presidio captain sought permission to move his garrison to Los Almagres (Presidio San Luis de las Amarillas), in order to work the mine and obtained ore samples. He calculated a yield of one and one half ounces of silver from seventy-five pounds of ore.

The San Sabá Mission was destroyed by hostile Indians on 16 March 1758. The presidio captain, Ortiz Parrilla, was reassigned

---

[171] Eckhardt, C.F. 1982. *The Lost San Sabá Mines*. Austin, Texas: Texas Monthly Press. p 35.

[172] Ibid. Also see - Bolton, Herbert Eugene. 1915. *Texas in the Middle Eighteenth Century: Studies in Spanish Colonial History and Administration*. Berkeley, California: University of California Press. Also see - Weddle, Robert S. Weddle. 1964. *The San Sabá Mission*. Austin, Texas: University of Texas Press.

[173] Eckhardt, C.F. 1982. *The Lost San Sabá Mines*. Austin, Texas: Texas Monthly Press. pp 39-40.

and the mine was never opened. Parrilla's interest, combined with Miranda's report, gave birth to an enduring legend.

On 28 February 1758 Toribio de Guevara reported that the seventy-five pound sample of ore yielded one and one half ounces of silver, which Guevera delivered to Don José de Ecay Muzquiz.[174]

The slag heap left behind by the Spaniards on the bank of the San Sabá River gave later treasure seekers a false clue, causing them to believe that the mine to be in that area. Interest in the mine continued to surface from time to time throughout the colonial period. Governor Barón de Ripperdá sent an expedition to examine the mines in 1778. Once again, ore samples were extracted and sent for analysis. In 1788–89 a Frenchman named Alexandre Dupont extracted ore samples from the site and took them to Mexico for assay. He made a follow up trip to the mine site, circling as far north perhaps as the Red River and into present day Oklahoma. DuPont returned to San Antonio, but never to the mine site called "Honey Creek." In the summer of 1789 six men left San Antonio, headed to the mine to work the deposit. Apaches attacked the group and killed all but one.

In 1810 Jose Maria Garcia wrote in his letter to Provincial Governor Don Manuel Salcedo that Indians had taken silver from the mine and made jewelry from it.[175] Garcia had visited the site, and his military escort Lieutenant Don Juan Padillo carved his name in the archway at the entrance to the Presidio San Luis de las Amarillas, inscribing "Padillo 1810."[176]

Two years later, in 1812, Don Ignacio Obregon, royal mine inspector, speaks of richness of the mine, and the fact that the mine is in an area that none would suspect, hidden by limestone rock formations.[177]

In more recent years geologists have added to the mystique of the mine legend, claiming that there is an underground river running parallel to the San Saba, and that after a significant rise

---

[174] Nathan, Paul D. translator. Forward by Weddle, Robert S.. 2000. *The San Sabá Papers*. Dallas, Texas: Southern Methodist University Press. p 143.
[175] Desmond, H.A. 1976. *My Search for Las Almagres Mine, Later Called Bowie's Mine*. Bi-Centenial Edition 1976. Pages not numbered.
[176] Ibid.
[177] Ibid.

occasioned by heavy rainfall some of the purest gold ore imaginable has been recovered. The same geologists claim to have found local sites where the Spanish may have used quicksilver to process gold ore.[178]

When Stephen F. Austin arrived in Texas he heard stories about the lost mine and sent soldiers to investigate. They probably went to the wrong place. By 1829 stories of the "lost" silver mine of San Sabá began appearing on Austin's maps. For years afterward it was mentioned in nearly every book about Texas.

When James and Rezin Bowie marched into the Hill Country, pushing their real estate scheme of selling unwitting suckers land in hostile Indian country, their presence reinforced the old legend. The Bowies already had a reputation for fronting land schemes, having sold fraudulent claims in Arkansas Territory and masterminding a property swindle in Louisiana.[179] On balance, historians have treated James Bowie, who was a hero of the Alamo, far more kindly than certain elements of his past might otherwise dictate. But besmirching the standing of Bowie is not the point. Offering the proposition that his role in the Los Almagres mine story might be more myth than fact is, however.

A Lipan Indian Chief named Xolic is said to have led the Bowies to the site, where "…the men could literally have cut slabs of silver out of the vein with their belt knives…"[180] Los Almagres was transformed into the "lost San Saba mine," then the "lost Bowie mine." Caiphas K. Ham, a sporadic associate to the Bowie brothers claimed that he, not James Bowie, was told of a mine rich in silver. Ham claimed, Rezin Bowie, not James Bowie, saw Spanish bars of silver tucked away in a mine. Ham continued to search long after Colonel Bowie's death at the fall of the Alamo. In a letter by E. McLean to Caiphas K. Ham dated 8 December 1880, McLean warns Ham to keep knowledge of the mine to himself.

---

[178] Desmond, H.A. 1976. *My Search for Las Almagres Mine, Later Called Bowie's Mine*. Bi-Centenial Edition 1976. Pages not numbered.

[179] Wallis, Michael. 2011. *David Crockett, The Lion of the West*. W.W. Norton. New York, New York: p 297.

[180] Ibid. pp 12-13.

There has been practically as much written about James and Rezin P. Bowie's search for the Los Almagres as there has been about the mines themselves. Detractors wonder if the Bowies really searched at all? Most believe that James Bowie in particular, was never in the vicinity of the mine at all…period![181] On the other hand, the fact that what many historians believe is an authentic signature of James Bowie, signed "bouie" as it should be, is carved into the rock edifice of the Presidio San Luis de las Amarillas does tend to support the fact that the famous knife fighter may well have passed through the country.

As for how James Bowie came by his silver bars, some believe that he stole them. Bowie had married the daughter of the vice-governor of Coahulia. When she died he dropped into the gutter and immersed himself in booze for about two years, according to the legend, spending the silver on drink.

James Bowie also claimed to have lived among the Lipan Indians. There simply isn't enough time between Bowie's famed Vidalia Sandbar Fight and the death of his wife for this story to be true. One always finds reference to the Bowie Party's encountering roughly one hundred and sixty Indians, the tally of hostiles depends upon which account one reads. In any case, The Battle of Calf Creek took place on Monday, 21 November 1831. James and Rezin Bowie, Caiphas (Cephas) K. Ham (Hamm), Robert Armstrong, David Buchanan, Mathew Doyle (Doyal), Jesse Wallace, Thomas McCaslin, James Coryell, two servants, a Mexican named Gonzales and a mulatto boy named Charles are known to have been involved in the 1831 affray. Other sources claim between fourteen and twenty-five men were involved in the battle.[182]

---

[181] Ibid. pp 101-103.
[182] Ibid. p 101.

**Signature of James Bowie at Presidio San Luis de las Amarillas
Menard, Texas**
Photo from Author's Collection

The exact site of the battle remains a question with some historians, as does Bowie's involvement in the mine legend. Conjecture is endless. The fable often runs afoul of accepted history. It is difficult for one to separate the circumstantial evidence, history, legend, and physical evidence. Rezin Bowie said the battle occurred "six miles east of the old fort." That would place it near Jackson's Creek. Some local historians and storytellers believe it was near Silver Creek, which is nine miles west and three miles north of the old presidio. Author Bill Townsley writes that in the 1860s Dixon, G.B. Ezell, Wiley Stroud and Sam Fleming came to possess a map showing the location of a mine tunnel on Silver Creek. The area is commonly referred to as the Egg-Shaped Basin, or Llano Basin by some. There's a wash known as Turkey Creek that some consider the correct location of the fight. The state of Texas seems to prefer a site near Calf Creek, a tributary of the San Saba River, however. Such controversy is not uncommon in this, and many other contentious historical matters. In any case, there is a great deal of physical evidence to ponder.

In the early 1900s Herbert E. Bolton, accompanied by J. Farley of Dallas, traveled to the alleged mine location and opened what has become known as the Boyd shaft on Honey Creek. Farley formed the Los Almagres Mining Company. In 1909 members of the United States Geological Survey visited the site and described the mine as being "unproductive." Some, however, dispute the correctness of this location, claiming the mine is elsewhere. At least one local historian who has studied the topic for a lifetime contends that the site is not in Menard County at all.[183]

None-the-less, Bolton's claim of having found the lost San Sabá mine has not deterred the romantics. Although the *Texas Almanac* published a lengthy article on the subject in 1996-1997, few people are aware that the site of the "lost mission" is not lost, and was located in September 1993 in a hay filed about four miles east of the old presidio.

Local Menard County old timers will volunteer that the countryside is peppered with sites bearing silver ore deposits, but are closed-lipped when asked where an enterprising prospector might begin a search. Thus, those who prefer an elegant legend to historical verity continue to explore the mineral bearing rock of Menard County. Untold hours and fortune have been squandered in quest of the lost mine called La Mina de las Almagres.

---

[183] Desmond, H.A. 1976. *My Search for Las Almagres Mine, Later Called Bowie's Mine*. Bi-Centenial Edition 1976. Pages not numbered.

Chapter VI

Menardville

Only those Americans who are willing to die for their country are fit to live.[184]
Douglas MacArthur

Deciding what material to include in a book, and what to pass over, is a dilemma faced by all authors. In the case of *Fort McKavett, and Tales of Menard County* the matter was uniquely perplexing. Menardville is located less than thirty miles east of Fort McKavett, which is the focal point of this book. It is the county seat of Menard County, and in many ways its history is inexorably linked to that of Fort McKavett. Neglecting to offer the reader adequate reference to Menard would have been a colossal oversight. On the other hand, the history of Menardville is so extensive that it should be covered in a book of its own. The 1982 publication titled *Menard County History, An Anthology* printed by Anchor Publishing contains 784 pages.[185] Another fine reference is the book titled *The Free State of Menard*, containing 213 pages of data on Menard County.[186] Much of that text of both books is devoted to Menardville itself. Thus given the limitations of this manuscript, the author has been left with the ageless task of choosing how to divide the baby – so to speak. Having complete confidence that what few tales of Menardville history I have chosen to cover will inevitably turn

---

[184] Menard, Texas holds the distinction of having sent more men off to fight in WWII, as a percent of population, than any other town in the United States.

[185] Menard County Historical Society. 1982. *Menard County History, An Anthology*. San Angelo, Texas: Anchor Publishing.

[186] Pierce, N.H. 1946. *The Free State of Menard, A History of the County*. Menard, Texas: Menard News Press.

out to be the wrong ones for some stern inhabitants I press on...regardless.

The area surrounding Menardville was used as a camp by Indians and a landmark for expeditions in search of a legendary silver mine dating to the era of Spanish exploration in the 1700s. An Apache encampment housing upwards of 3,000 Indians was located not far from the townsite. Favorable terrain, abundant water, fuel and game supported a sizeable Native population for thousands of years, and evidence of their inhabitation is abundant. That Native residency, in fact, may be the real story of the Menardville area considering that it dates to the Paleo-Indian period, making the occupation by Anglo settlers akin to a flyspeck on the timeline of history.

To begin with, the unique geology of the Edwards Plateau, covering approximately 30,000 square miles in total, allowed the natural production of a mineral quartz rock called Edwards Chert. Chert, or flint as it is more commonly called, was the lithic material used by the early inhabitants for tools and weapons.[187] The Lithic stage was the earliest period of human occupation in the Americas, occurring during the Late Pleistocene period, earlier than 10,000 years ago. The stage derived its name from the first appearance of stone tools. The highly valued local Edwards chert was traded by Indians over distances as remote as 600 miles.[188] The foregoing explains, in part, the tremendous array of Indians who made their home in this region. Although remains and evidence of early inhabitants dates back to the Early Paleo period, 12,000-13,000 years ago, the inhabitants who came into contact with Spanish explorers and early settler were from the Late Prehistoric Austin and Toyah Phase, dating back 400 years or more, and the relatively recent Proto Historical and Historical era, covering 50 to 400 years prior.[189]

---

[187] Lithic means of or pertaining to stone. In archaeology, lithic artifacts include ground and chipped stone tools and the debris resulting from their manufacture.
[188] Bryant Saner. 17 September 2011. Hill Country Archaeology Society.
[189] Ibid.

The town was originally called Menardville when the site was laid out in 1858. That year three families inhabited the site and lived in log cabins surrounded by split-log palisades.

When nearby Fort McKavett closed in 1859, residents were left to protect themselves from the all too frequent Indian depredations that plagued the district. When the fort reopened in April 1868 settlers were once again attracted to the region.

By 1867 Menardville had a store operated by Adam Bradford in a one-room log house, a blacksmith shop, a saloon and grocery. Supplies had to be freighted overland from Burnet. Menardville served the region as a trading post and later an overnight stop on north and west cattle trails. The old Presidio San Luis de las Amarillas compound just west of town was used as a holding area for cattle.[190]

In the early 1870s the construction of an irrigation ditch to facilitate crop production in the vicinity of Menardville was a welcome boost to agriculture. The Vaughn Agricultural and Mechanical Canal Company was chartered in 1874 by William J. Vaughn, president; William Tipton, director; and James H. Comstock, Director and secretary. Major H.M. Holmes was appointed attorney. Irrigation for 2,000 acres of valley cropland and hydropower for gristmills was furnished by the gravity flow of water from the San Saba River. Use of the irrigation canal, called "The Ditch", which runs for five miles above town to five miles below, began in 1876. Vaughn sold his controlling interest to Gus Noyes in 1886. Since 1905 "The Ditch" has been operated by Menard Irrigation Company, still using the original dam from circa 1874.[191]

According to field notes by surveyor John Dexter, who surveyed the waterway's route in 1875, portions of the main canal of 1874 follow the original path of the Spanish *acequia*, which dates to between 1757 and 1772. Dexter's survey makes note of the exact point where the new canal tied into the Old

---

[190] Menard County Historical Society. 1982. *Menard County History-An Anthology*. San Angelo, Texas: Anchor.

[191] Texas State Historical Marker. *The Ditch*. 1972. Marker Number 5327000012.

Spanish Ditch.[192] The original plan for the ditch had included an additional fifteen miles of waterway.

Although certainly not to the scale of the aqueducts of the Roman Empire, the Menardville ditch was quite an accomplishment for 1874 rural Texas, and facilitated much improved crop production and ranching in the region. Some Menardville visitors might not be impressed without understanding the history of "The Ditch", such as a recent Californian transplanted to Texas who commented "What can you say about a town whose main attraction is a ditch?"[193] A great deal would be my reply.

Lucrative trade from Buffalo Soldiers billeted at Fort McKavett came to an end in June 1883 when the fort closed for good. By the mid-1880s the community boasted 150 residents with a church, school, and several stores. Residents derived their income largely from trade in livestock, wool, and hides. Early newspapers included the Menardville *Monitor*, founded by William Columbus Redman in 1887. As has been the case since the origin of the written word, another paper called the *Record* was established in 1889, probably to hold forth an alternate point of view. The *Enterprise* followed in 1892 (some cite 1893), and the *Messenger* in 1908.

For Menardville residents, floods have been all to frequent over the years. Most have been no more than a temporary inconvenience, often looked upon as a blessing considering the semi-arid Texas countryside. Others have been catastrophic to citizens, crops and livestock. During one such episode Menardville flooded, literally from hilltop to hilltop, in the epic deluge of 1899. An article in one local newspaper provides a gripping recollection of the events as they unfolded that day:

> It was rather a surprise that Monday's dawn did not witness a freshet in the stream at Menardville, but we did not have long to wait. By eight o'clock the rise began, and in less than four hours the waters were out of bank and flooding crops in the valley. It soon began falling, however,

---

[192] Archeological Studies Branch of the Environmental Affairs Division and the San Angelo District Office, Texas Department of Transportation. *The Menard Irrigation Canal.* Prewitt and Associates. 2007.
[193] Matthew High. San Antonio, Texas. Flickr Post. 29 March 2008.

and fell as rapidly as it rose, and many supposed the danger was past. Still heavy clouds hung over the head waters and occasional showers continued to fall along the valley. Some crops were badly damaged even then. It was still early in the afternoon, when the river began to rise again, and the thoughtful people commenced preparing for a speedy evacuation of the valley. By six o'clock the big rise was coming through the town but the upward movement was so slow that it was still hoped that the danger would pass and many even retired to sleep, and were rudely awakened by the cries of the more cautious and watchful that the town was flooded and the waters still rising.[194]

Then followed a scene of confusion, which may be understood by those who have experienced the effect on similar occasions. Every man and boy in town turned out to the rescue of the helpless, and although they saw their own property swept away and destroyed, nothing was attempted to save it, until every woman, child and old man in the town was removed to a point of safety. There were deeds of heroism and self-sacrifice that will long be remembered and mentioned after this generation has passed away--but this is not the time to speak of them.

Several, after seeing the helpless out of danger returned to see after their own interest, only to find their business houses gone, and learn that they were financially ruined.[195]

The disaster resulted in considerable damage, but resolute citizens rebuilt the following year.

Continued growth permitted the establishment of the town's first bank in 1903. With the impending arrival of the Fort Worth and Rio Grande Railroad Company the community was asked to rename their fine town "Menard" in order to facilitate the painting of signs. (Fortunately the Fort Worth and Rio Grande Railroad was not confronted with the challenge of renaming the town of Lake Chaubunagungamaug in Massachusetts, it boasting the longest place name in the United States.)[196]

---

[194] *Menard News and Messenger.* 18 June 1936.
[195] Ibid.
[196] The actual forty-five letter place name of the town is Lake Chargoggagoggmanchauggagoggchaubunagungamaugg. See Trumbull, James Hammond. 1881. *Indian Names of Places etc., In and On the Borders of Connecticut: With interpretations of Some of Them.* Reprinted in facsimile 1974 under title *Indian Names in Connecticut.* Hamden, Connecticut: Archon Books.

With the aid of incentives offered by the county including a right-of-way, land for stock pens and depot, and $10,000 to build the station itself, the Fort Worth and Rio Grande Railroad Company extended its track to Menardville. In February 1911 the first train arrived. With the addition of rail service, citizens of the region could reach outside markets easier.[197]

With the arrival of the "iron horse" Menard experienced an economic boom. By 1914 the town boasted two banks and a variety of businesses. The population grew to 1,000.

The Atchison, Topeka and Santa Fe Railway discontinued service to Menard in 1972 and donated the old depot to the county for use as a history museum.[198] The population grew to 1,697 by 1980 and has remained at about that level since. Inhabitants of the county have been shrinking at a rate of about 5% in recent years.[199]

---

[197] Menard County Historical Society. 1982. *Menard County History-An Anthology*. San Angelo, Texas: Anchor.

[198] The Menard County Historical Society began collecting artifacts in 1975 and dedicated the museum in 1978.

[199] 2010 United States Census. Menard County, Texas. Population 2,242. Source U.S. Census Bureau: State and County QuickFacts.

Engineer John C. Clark (left) – Menardville Station
Courtesy of the Menardville Museum
Photo from Author's Collection

The Iron Clad Saloon – Menardville, Texas – Circa
Courtesy of the Menardville Museum

In its heyday Menard boasted nine saloons, including the Cottonwood, Legal Tender, Road to Ruin, Ironclad, Rock Saloon, Erskin & Bevans saloon and the Gay Brothers Saloon.[200] That may seem like a lot of drinking establishments for such a small community but one must take into consideration the fact that the surrounding communities were "dry" during the early days, contributing greatly to the hustle and bustle on the streets of Menard.

Buffalo Soldiers from nearby Fort McKavett frequented Menardville while off duty, bringing with them much desired trade and dollars. Although their money was always welcome there, the soldiers' presence was only "tolerated," and not eagerly enjoyed by all. Post Civil War Texas under Republican rule by "Yankee Carpetbaggers" was not yet a welcoming and diverse setting. Many locals had lost family and friends during the recent hostilities and were not quite ready to roll out the welcome mat to the victors. None-the-less, the troops came to

---

[200] In 1881 Sergeant William Johnston opened the Rock Saloon at Menardville. He later became one of the town's leading citizens.

Menardville to drink away the boredom and loneliness. According to local folklore, at the end of a long evening of revelry the soldiers would take a whiskey bottle with them and begin the long walk back to Fort McKavett. Along the route home when they had drained the vessel of John Barleycorn they would write notes on small pieces of paper and insert them into the bottles, casting the containers off into "The Ditch" where the flowing water would carry the bottles to points east where they were later discovered by curious locals.[201]

As cited earlier, Indian depredations had been on the rise during the Civil War years. The presence of federal troops aided in curbing the threat, but much of the work still fell to the Texas Rangers. Rangers had a huge presence in Menard County, fighting Indians as well as chasing desperados. The era of the big cattle drives north to Kansas and west to New Mexico also ushered in a time of unbridled lawlessness for many parts of Texas.

---

[201] John Kniffen to Clifford R. Caldwell. 15 September 2011.

The Legal Tender Saloon – Menardville, Texas – circa 1890
Courtesy of the Menardville Museum

Rounding up stray "maverick" cattle on the open range was okay, but cattle rustling was not. You could get away with murder in Menard County, but not cattle rustling. Some malefactors came to discover the truth of that idiom at the knotted end of a stout hemp rope. Unemployed cowboys and returning Confederate soldiers who came home to find that they had lost everything they had often took to crime as a means of making a living. Such noted bandits and gunmen as

Rube Boyce, the McKeevers, John Ringo and the Dublin Gang all spent time in the area. Texas Rangers based on Bear Creek in neighboring Kimble County conducted a large-scale roundup in 1877 and brought numerous criminals to justice.

Texas Ranger records from that era speak to a ranger camp on the San Saba:

Camp near Menardville
August 25th 1876
Gen. Order No. 10:
Co. AF will be stationed on the San Saba river about midway between Menardville & Fort McKavett in Menard County. Post & Telegraph office Ft. McKavett.

Again later the same month:

Headquarters Frontier Battalion
Camp Menite Kerr. Co. Texas
Aug. 29th 1876
Gen. Order No. 11:
Co. AD will be stationed on the San Saba river about midway between Fort McKavett and Menardville in Menard County. Post and Telegraph office Ft. McKavett Care of Sam Wallack.

Other records reveal that Ranger Captain Dan W. Roberts' Company D was camped at Little Saline Creek at the edge of Menard County in 1875.[202] Roberts issued a call to increase the number of rangers in the area to fifty men, and began recruiting efforts at Menardville. Among those who signed on were nearby residents Lamartine Pemberton "Lam" and Edward Armon "Ed" Sieker and James Buchanan "Jim" Gillette, taking the oath on 1 July 1875.[203] After a busy summer, Roberts' men set up their winter camp for 1875-1876 on the San Saba River, below Menardville, building five cabins each about eighteen feet square.

---

[202] Desmond, H.A. 1976. *Texas Knights of the Hill Country, Story of the Texas Rangers.* Bi-Centenial Edition 1976. Pages not numbered.
[203] Ibid.

Some problematic tavern visitors were neither Buffalo Soldier nor citizen. Texas Ranger were, on occasion, known to be at the root of a whiskey fueled disagreement gone fatally wrong. To that end the adjutant general instituted the following mandate:

Adjutant General's Office State of Texas Austin, Feby [February] 21, 1878. General Order No. 25:
As heretofore directed State troops will lay aside their arms when in cities or towns, unless in the discharge of some specific duty.
Visiting saloons, circuses or other places of amusement with arms, unless under an order for a specific purpose, is forbidden.
By command of Governor R. B. Hubbard Commander in Chief [signed] Wm Steele Adjutant General

Gravesite of Texas Ranger Edward Armon Sieker
Pioneer Rest Cemetery – Menardville
Photo from Author's Collection

Emil Toepperwein's Photographic Studio – Menardville - circa 1895
Photo Courtesy of the Menardville Museum

Emil Toepperwein Saddlery – Menardville, Texas – circa 1900
Courtesy of the Menardville Museum

In spite of the excitement brought about by outlaws, intoxicated troopers and local revelers the town of Menardville thrived. Like all of Texas, the depression of the 1930s hit Menardville residents hard, however Menard National Bank and the Bevans State Bank remained opened and most Menard residents managed to recover. A gradual shift in agriculture away from cotton took place, and in post depression years emphasis shifted more toward livestock. About 96 percent of agricultural receipts came from livestock and livestock products, the most important ones being sheep, wool, cattle, angora goats, and mohair.

Emil Toepperwein was among the early entrepreneurs of Menardville. Toepperwein was born 31 January 1870 at Fredericksburg, son of Herman and Amelia Toepperwein. As a young man he apprenticed with noted saddle-maker Ben Varas and experimented with his interest in photography, Later Emil worked for A. A. Brack who owned a thriving photography business in San Antonio. After only one year's experience with Brack, Emil began traveling to local communities applying his skills as a photographer.

Toepperwein settled at Menard circa 1895 and opened a photographic studio along with a saddlery to augment his income. The saddle and harness business soon consumed all of Emil's time. He hired one of his brothers, Ed, to help him meet the demand. Fritz Luckenbach, who was now Emil's brother-in-law, owned the building Emil used for the saddlery. In 1903 the two men formed a partnership and built another store called the Luckenbach Hardware Company that was connected to the saddle shop.[204] Examples of Toepperwein's leather work are highly sought after by collectors today.

In 1912, Emil expanded his business and applied to the Ford Motor Co. for a dealership, which he was awarded this in 1915. At the time of his retirement, he was the third oldest Ford dealer in Texas.

On the long list of noted Menardville residents is Noah Hamilton Rose. Rose was a printer, photographer and collector of photographs of the frontier West. Rose was born seventy-

---

[204] Alicia Brown. "Emil Toepperwein." *The Texas GenWeb Project*. 22 March 2008.

five miles northwest of San Antonio in Kendall County on 9 April 1874. In 1884 his father, who was a carpenter, moved his family to Menardville where Noah was educated and in 1888 began working as an apprentice in the office of the Menardville Monitor. In 1901, Rose's photographic work focused on hangings, shootouts, gunmen, sheriffs, politicians and judges. Soon he began seeking old photographs of noted personalities. In 1904, Rose set up a photography studio in Del Rio, and worked to build his collection of photographs.

J.H. "Jim" Cannon with Mule Wagon in front of Menardville Jail circa 1911
Photo Courtesy of Menardville Museum

In 1921, Rose moved to San Antonio. After suffering a long illness he found himself in debt for medical bills. To salvage his business he printed a catalogue of the negatives of his collection and developed a successful mail-order business selling photographs to magazines and collectors. He eventually collected over 2,000 photographs. His collection of photographs is now in the collection of the University of Oklahoma at Norman.

There is a lone gravesite situated east of Menardville on FM 2092, just off the highway under a stand of trees. The site consists of a solitary headstone, standing boldly erect and protected by an iron fence, which seems to be guarding it from nothing more threatening than nature itself. The inscription on the tablet reads "No pain, no grief, no anxious fear; Can reach the peace for Sleeper Here". The monument marks the burial location of Tullius (Tullos) B. "Tully" Smith, born 14 January 1833 and died 10 January 1871. Although perhaps not one of Menardville's most prominent citizens "Tully" Smith's story has captivated this author.

Tullius B. Smith was one of the thirteen children of Saul G. Smith and Talitha Dobson.[205] He married Cynthia B. Russell on 11 April 1857 at Fannin County, Texas. By 1870 "Tully" Smith had removed to Menard County where he is listed on the census as a "store-keeper".[206] Living in his household were his wife Cynthia, two daughters (Lucilla A. & Brooklin), two sons (Robert S. & Alijah) and his father Saul G. Smith.[207]

Smith was apparently a partner of Pat Mires before he opened his own store. The house he and his family lived in was a one-room log wall structure, covered with four foot boards that had been split from the giant oak trees that grew plentiful at the time along the San Saba River bottoms. Smith also ran a post office.[208]

According to local legend Smith had worked for a man named Peter Robertson who claimed that:

> *Tull Smith, the last named being a young man who before that had worked for me and had been severely bitten by a wolf. We were in camp one night and while he was asleep, the wolf came prowling around and approaching his pallet, seized his hand and mangled it badly before he*

---

[205] Ancestry. Tree 27132795. Person 1997819470.
[206] US Census. Census Year 1870. Census Place Menard, Texas. Roll M593_1594. Page 159B. Image 322. Family History Library Film 553093.
[207] Ibid.
[208] Alicia Brown. "Tull B. Smith." *TxGenWeb Project*. 22 March 2008

could get loose. He said he could have shot the wolf but was afraid Indians might hear the gun and hurt him worse than the wolf.

Robertson also claimed that Smith had been locked up by Colonel Ranald Mackenzie's troops at Fort McKavett for suspicion of aiding "Humpy" Jackson in his escape after the "Lanky Jim" affair.

At the time of his death locals claimed that "Tully" Smith was killed by Indians. However, the general consensus of provincial folklore is that the Indian story was a cover up for a dastardly deed done by others. Smith had closed up his store that Tuesday night, 10 January 1871, and left with a bag of money. He was ambushed by a group of robbers who shot him with guns, then put arrows in the bullet holes to make it look as though he fell victim to an Indian attack. Although such attacks by hostiles were by no means uncommon, Indians rarely stole a victim's boots and moneybag, which were both missing when "Tully's" body was discovered.

In *The West Texas Frontier* author Joseph Carroll McConnell describes "Tully's" death as follows:

> *Tullos [Tullius] B. Smith was returning late in the evening to his home in Menard, from the Wilkerson Ranch, about sixteen miles away, was mounted on a large black pony, and was leading about two other horses. As he passed a cluster of bushes, a few miles from his destination, Tullos [Tullius] B. Smith was ambushed and killed. Late in the evening the stage going from San Antonio to El Paso came along and found him. Since he was not scalped, some local citizens thought perhaps he may [might] not have been killed by Indians. Searching parties soon found moccasin tracks, however, and other Indian signs. Wm. Templeton, Lewis Wilson and David Thorp brought Tullos [Tullius] B. Smith's body to Menard in a spring wagon.*[209]

The data seems inconclusive, however, the rest of the story is intriguing. Most curious is the fact that the author, McConnell,

---

[209] McConnell, Joseph Carroll. 1933. *The West Texas Frontier, or A Descriptive History Of Early Times In Western Texas, Containing an Accurate Account Of Much Hitherto Unpublished History.* Jacksboro & Palo Pinto.

gleaned his account from J.F.P. Kruse. Kruse was either "Tully" Smith's partner or employee. On 26 August 1872, just one year after Smith's death, he married "Tully's" grieving widow, Cynthia.

As cited earlier, Menardville deserves to have a book written exclusively about its unique past. There is much more to the rich history, and folklore, of Menardville. Hopefully history buffs will think enough of the few tales that this author has shared and visit the community to investigate for themselves.

Gravesite of Tullius B. Smith – Menard, Texas
Photo from Author's Collection

Chapter VII

Hext, Callan & Saline

> *Thus let me live, unseen, unknown,*
> *Thus unlamented let me die; Steal from the world,*
> *and not a stone Tell where I lie.*
> **Alexander Pope**

Many readers, including this author, find the history of the scores of small towns that have vanished from the Lone Star landscape to be especially fascinating. Today's travelers on the Texas back roads often do so with the windows rolled up tight, air conditioner running full out, stereo wide open...not knowing that they are speeding past the site of a once thriving and expectant little community. At least three such locales grace the landscape of Menard County...Hext, Callan and Saline.

Hext

The modest community of Hext is located at the intersection of State Highway 29 and Farm Road 1221, sixteen miles southeast of Menard in eastern Menard County. Hext was once known as Maringo, or Marengo, when the area was settled in the 1870s. Residents changed the name to Hext in the late 1890s in honor of Joseph Robert Hext.[210]

According to some sources the town was named after the two Hext brothers in 1895. The switch occurred when residents applied for a post office and discovered that the name "Maringo" had already been taken. Thus the first mail facility was established, and called Hext, in 1897. Unfortunately, 144 years later the Hext post office is on the 2011 U.S. Postal Service list of locations to be closed. Ennis Stark was

---

[210] Menard County Historical Society. 1982. *Menard County History-An Anthology.* San Angelo, Texas: Anchor.

postmaster. Joseph Robert "Bob" Hext married to Lettie Anderson in 1884 and moved to what was then Marengo in about 1888. His brother, James Bruten Hext, moved with him and married a woman named Amanda (surname unknown). Together they started a rather large ranch in Menard County. Some historians have claimed that for reasons unknown James moved his family to Oklahoma in the early 1890s.

One can easily speculate that a move from west Texas in the 1890s might have been a consequence of the extended drought that plagued the region during that period. James Hext and his wife Amanda appear on census documents for Menard County, Texas in 1900, Gray County, Texas in 1910 and Roosevelt County, New Mexico in 1920, thus adding further confusion to the saga. James Hext died in 1931. Brother Robert remained in the area (Menard, Mason, Schleicher and Burnet Counties) until his death in 1941.[211]

However, according to some sources the town of Hext may have had as many as four names over the years. Some local historians contend that after the town was first called Marengo it was renamed Peg Leg Pocket. According to legend there was a peg-leg man who lived on the river nearby. The hills around the town slope down toward an old river crossing forming a pocket, thus the name Peg Leg Pocket. Another source claims that the town name was changed to Wagoner Ville when Lee Wagoner operated a store there. Later, when the post office was moved, the name was changed to Hext.[212] George Henry Wagoner's 1956 obituary does claim that he built the first house and commercial building in Hext, which became a store. However, no mention is made of Wagoner Ville appears in any other reference material the author has uncovered.

In 1914 the community boasted a cotton gin, hotel, two general stores and 125 residents. A Church of Christ congregation was organized in 1904, and a Baptist church established in 1916. By the mid-1920s the population of the community had fallen to forty. In the late 1940s it rose to sixty,

---

[211] Ancestry Files. Tree #7859263. Person # 784531604
[212] *Menard News*. 9 March 1939

then remained at that level through the mid-1980s. The community reported seventy- three residents in 2000.

Callan

Callan was located ten miles northeast of Menardville, in northeastern Menard County. In 1908 seventy-five year old James Joseph Callan, a local landowner who had come to the United States from Dundalk, County Louth Ireland, gave the Fort Worth and Rio Grande Railroad Company a site for a depot and several miles of right-of-way crossing his land.[213,214] Callan was in the newspaper business for a number of years at Coleman. He continued his writing after moving to Menard. Callan served as Commissioner of Menard County and for twenty years and held the office of Justice of the Peace at the time of his death. He had acquired the 1,242.75 acres of land by means of a Texas School Lands act on 14 July 1899.[215]

The track connecting Brady and Menard was completed in July 1911, and the Richey-DeFreest Land Company formed the Callan City Company to build a stopover community along the path of the new railroad. The company bought 542 acres from James J. Callan and his wife Margaret, and divided the parcel

---

[213] US Census. Census Year: 1900. Census Place Justice Precinct 1, Menard, Texas. Roll T623_1657. Page 7B. Enumeration District 62.

[214] Citing - *The Menard Messenger* . Volume 10. Number 48. Thursday, 11 October 1917. p 1. "Another Pioneer Gone to Rest". After an illness lasting about three weeks, James J. [Joseph] Callan answered the call and passed to the great beyond. James J. Callan was born in Dundalk, Ireland, May 6, 1833 and died October 4, 1917. At the age of eleven he moved with his parents to America. The family lived in Washington, D. C. and it was there he received most of his schooling, spending several years and graduating in the Georgetown University.

On March 13, 1859 he was married to Margaret M. Sheen at Camp Colorado, Texas, at which time he was in the United States Army, but shortly after was sent to the Mexican border where he served for one year.

For a number of years he was in the newspaper business at Coleman and after moving to Menard continued his writing until he became too feeble.

Mr. Callan for several years served as Commissioner of Menard County and for the past twenty years has been Justice of the Peace, this office he was holding at the time of his death.

[215] Texas General Land Office. Abstracts of all original Texas Land Titles comprising Grants and Locations. Austin, Texas. Certificate 108. File 43767.

into town lots. At its peak the Callan community had a hotel, a general store, a lumberyard, and a livery stable and wagon yard to complement the stockyards that the railroad company had built. Plans were made to open a bank, but the idea was abandoned when a drought threatened the local economy. A post office was in operation at Callan in 1911 to 1912, and again from 1915 to 1919. Population estimates for the Callan area in the 1920s ranged from fifty to seventy-five. The town's namesake, James J. Callan, died on 4 October 1917.[216] He is buried at the Pioneer Rest Cemetery at Menard.

Over time travelers were able to cover greater distances by automobile on improved thoroughfares of the new century. Communities like Callan soon became obsolete and were progressively abandoned. Most of the old buildings at Callan were vacant, and fell victim to the scrap metal drives for the war effort in the early 1940s. The school at Callan closed for good in 1939. By 1940 only a few scattered houses marked the remnants of the little community. By 1880 virtually all traces of its existence had disappeared.[217]

Today one can reach what remains of Callan by traveling east on Highway 190 from Menard, then turning north on Callan Lane. One's journey will not be rewarding, however. Callan is on private property, and access is by permission only. Practically no evidence of the early town remains.

Saline

A few brave pioneers settled Saline in the 1860s, but the constant threat of Indian depredations kept all but the most resolute folks away until Fort McKavett was reopened in 1868. The family of Henry Parks was among the early group of hale Texans to settle near Saline, where they found abundant grazing for their cattle. During one of the all too frequent Indian raids, a band of Comanches descended on the Parks family in the summer the spring of 1862, killing Henry and Nancy Parks as well as their young grandson, Billy. Their home was burned and

---

[216] Texas Department of Health. Texas Death Indexes. 1903-2000. Austin, Texas. Texas Department of Health. State Vital Statistics Unit.
[217] Citing - Menard County Historical Society. 1982. *Menard County History-An Anthology*. San Angelo, Texas: Anchor.

their livestock driven off. Stephen "Steve" Caviness, who was later killed near Fort McKavett on 13 April 1870 in connection with the "Humpy" Jackson episode, was among the scouts who engaged in an Indian fight that took place near Saline on 2 April 1862. The incident stemmed from the tragic massacre of the Parks family.

Following the characteristic practice of the day, the Parks family was buried where they had been slain, and became the first settlers to be entombed at Saline.

James Joseph Callan
Photo Courtesy of James Bush - Ancestry

During the 1870s and 1880s intrepid homesteaders arrived, farming and ranching the rugged countryside. The small community grew, and by about 1900 the Saline school boasted eighty-four students and two teachers. The school and a church still marked the location of the old community on county highway maps in the late 1930s, but the classroom doors shut for good in 1947, and students were sent to London in neighboring Kimble County for their tutelage in "the three R's."

At the Little Saline Cemetery (at Saline) one will find the graves of Isaac Boyce, who died 7 May 1879, as well as four Civil War veterans -Asa Saunders, George W. Ake, James Amberson and William Brewer. Trail boss Samuel A. Hunter is also buried at Little Saline, all on a two acre grant executed by Ely I. Boyce for the purpose of building a school, church and cemetery.

By 1990 Saline reported fifty-eight residents. The citizenry held an annual homecoming at the community center that year. By 2000 the population had grown by one...to fifty-nine.[218]

The adventurous traveler can find Saline in southeastern Menard County. It can be reached by touring east from Highway 83 on Highway 29 to Hext, then south on Farm Road 1221 towards London for about ten miles.

---

[218] Citing Vivian Elizabeth Smyrl, "SALINE, TX." *Handbook of Texas*. See - Menard County Historical Society. 1982. *Menard County History-An Anthology*. San Angelo, Texas: Anchor.

Chapter VIII

The Buffalo Soldiers

There is a paradox in pride: it makes some men ridiculous, but prevents others from becoming so.
Charles Caleb Colton

The study of military history is one of the earliest and long enduring pursuits of scholars worldwide. Nations and their peoples have been at war literally since Cain picked up a rock and killed Abel. Recounting the brave deeds of exceptional military organizations brings honor to those who served, and inspires those who are yet to serve. Without question the service of black troops in the armies of the Unites States during virtually all wars beginning with the American Revolution has until recently gone unrecognized and unappreciated. When it comes to the men of the 41st, 24th and 25th Infantry and the 9th and 10th Cavalry, one must pause and ponder their world as it was in post Civil War Texas before forming an opinion concerning their contribution.

Slavery had been widespread since colonial times. Some abolitionists fought against the inhumane practice. Not until the issue rose to national theater as an adjunct to the underlying conflict over states' rights between northern, and predominantly slave holding southern states was the practice abolished. It would be decades before blacks were given equal rights and another century before a reasonable balance of equality became commonplace in America. How to handle the prickly topic of racial discrimination has been an ever-present undertow, and a curse, for all responsible historians researching and writing about the post Civil War reconstruction era.

Some of the black troops who fought during the post Civil War conflict, termed the Indian Wars, are commonly and often inaccurately referred to as "Buffalo Soldiers." Many were former slaves or sharecroppers, having been recently handed their freedom and an opportunity to join the military, receive a fair wage for their labor, and to bask in the prestige of wearing the uniform of the United States of America. These soldiers were often met with gratitude for their service by local citizens, rather than the prejudice they expected. One must imagine one's self in their place. Descendents of the black troops who served during the Indian Wars, and blacks in general, are entitled to recount these soldiers' accomplishments with great pride.

In recent decades there has been a wealth of material published about the Buffalo Soldiers. No paucity of information or shortage of opinion exists any longer. Most recent work tends to extol the virtues and accomplishments of these troops, in sharp contrast to earlier writing. So sharp is the contrast, and so absent the balance, that much of the contemporary material is of little value to the reader who wishes to form his or her own opinion. Champions of the Buffalo Soldiers center their writing on the legitimate achievements, but too often interject a savorless undertone of discrimination, despair and poor treatment. Detractors, on the other hand, often stretch to the opposite extreme, pointing out that as many black troops were killed in conflicts with citizens "off post" than died at the hand of hostile Indians during armed conflict.

The fact that Buffalo Soldiers were not readily accepted into largely rural, white, post Civil War Texas communities that were suffocating under Radical Republican Rule should not seems a conundrum to anyone. But the excessive consumption of intoxicating beverages by soldiers, and their involvement in the rowdy brawls that always seem to follow, is a phenomenon that knows no racial bounds and extends back as far back in time as the existence of the first military organizations. Thus the reader is left with the task of absorbing knowledge from two often diametrically opposed interpretations and attempting to strike a balance somewhere in the middle. As one noted historian remarked recently, "it is always best to form one's hypothesis after gathering the facts...not before."

During the Civil War more than 180,000 black soldiers saw service in segregated regiments in the Union Army. Although many of these outfits were not thrust into combat for a variety of reasons and biases of the day, some of the black units did earn outstanding combat records during the War Between the States. When Congress reorganized the regular army in the summer of 1866 for peacetime duties it recognized the military merits and accomplishments of the black soldiers by authorizing the formation of two regiments of black cavalry and six regiments of black infantry.

Henry Ossian Flipper – circa 1877

Further structural modifications were made to the black units in 1869 when the black infantry regiments, including the 41st, were consolidated into two units - the 24th United States Infantry and the 25th United States Infantry. The cavalry soldiers were organized into the 9th United States Cavalry and the 10th United States Cavalry. The two cavalry and two infantry regiments were comprised of all black enlisted men, and were commanded, almost without exception, by white officers. There were a few notable exceptions, however, such as the case of West Point graduate Henry Ossian Flipper. Flipper, who excelled in engineering and law, and was the first black man to attend the prestigious military academy. Flipper graduated in

1877 and, as a fledgling second lieutenant joined the ranks of the 10th Cavalry as a company grade officer.[219]

The early day of the new black regiments, such as the 9th, were difficult. In the midst of a cholera epidemic that was raging throughout New Orleans troops of the 9th were packed into a squalid and poorly ventilated building that had earlier served as a cotton bale factory. No stoves were provided, so the soldiers had to prepare their meals over open fires. As a result, twenty-nine troops died in a three month period between October and December 1866. Thirty of the men deserted by year-end, and were soon followed by sixteen more defectors.[220]

Lieutenant Grote Hutcheson's regimental history of the 9th cavalry characterized the new recruits as "woefully ignorant, entirely helpless," and that the ranks had been hastily filled by inferior men. Hutcheson went on to say that the black recruits "…though willing enough to learn, was difficult to teach."[221]

Colonel Benjamin Henry Grierson's 10th cavalry, posted at Fort Leavenworth was off to no better start than the 9th at New Orleans. Under the thumb of the prejudiced and petty commander General William Hoffman, Grierson's stay at the fort was made as uncomfortable as possible. Troopers were assigned to low ground that flooded during rainy periods. Many were hospitalized with pneumonia.[222]

The term "Buffalo Soldier" is said to have been coined by the Plains Indians. The designation generally applies to the four regiments of black troops who served, and more particularly to the two cavalry regiments that saw duty on the frontier in the post-Civil War years. The nomenclature or pseudonym was first applied to the 10th Cavalry, which was formed on 21 September

---

[219] The ranks of second lieutenant, first lieutenant and captain are considered company grade officers in the United States military services.

[220] Schubert, Frank N. 1997. *Black Valor, Buffalo Soldiers and the Medal of Honor 1870-1898*. Lanham, Maryland: Rowman & Littlefield Publishers, Inc. pp 11-12

[221] Edited by Theophilus Frances Rodenbrough. Bvt. Brigadier General and William L. Haskin. Major, First Artillery. 1896. *The Army of the United States. Historical Sketches of Staff and Line With Portraits of General-in-Chief.* Maynard, Merril & Co.

[222] Leckie, William H. and Leckie, Shirley A. 2003. *The Buffalo Soldiers, A Narrative of the Black Cavalry in the West.* Norman, Oklahoma: University of Oklahoma Press. p 14.

1866 at Fort Leavenworth, Kansas. As with most topics having to do with the Old West, sources feel compelled to disagree as to how the term "Buffalo Soldiers" came into popular use. According to the Buffalo Soldiers National Museum, the cognomen originated with the Cheyenne warriors during the winter of 1877. The actual Cheyenne translation is said to be "Wild Buffalo." However, author Walter Hill documented the account of Colonel Benjamin Grierson who founded the 10th Cavalry regiment and recalled that the nom de plume "Buffalo Soldier" was first used during an 1871 campaign against Comanches. [223]

The controversy does not end with the source and date of the term's first use however. That would be far too simple. Some claim that the nickname was given out of respect for the fierce fighting ability of the 10th cavalry troopers. Other assert that Indians called the black cavalry troops "Buffalo Soldiers" because of their dark curly hair, which resembled a buffalo's coat. There are those historians who claim that there is no evidence the black troopers perceived the term "Buffalo Soldier" as flattering.[224] Some found it insulting. Not wishing to leave any novelist out of the yarn, other historians have cleverly dodged the matter and point to a combination of both legends in their effort to espouse the most politically correct dogma. Whatever the case, the term "Buffalo Soldiers" became a universally accepted nomenclature for all black soldiers. The terminology is still used today by U.S. Army units that trace their lineage back to the 9th and 10th Cavalry units whose service earned them a place of honor in U.S. history.

From 1866 to the early 1890s the Buffalo Soldiers served at a variety of posts in Texas, the Southwest and the Great Plains. By the spring of 1869, the 41st Infantry and its commanding officer, Colonel Ranald S. Mackenzie arrived at Fort McKavett. As cited earlier, the 41st was later consolidated into the 24th and

---

[223] In 1873 the magazine *The Nation* is claimed to have been the first to use the term "Buffalo Soldier" adding further to the confusion of the origin. *Fort McKavett Gazette*. Volume 9 Number 5. May 2010.
[224] Weaver, John Downing. 1997. *The Senator and the Sharecropper's Son*. College Station, Texas: Texas A&M University Press. pp 212-213

25th infantry regiments. The 9th Cavalry was also Fort McKavett.

Much of the activity of the Buffalo Soldiers during the Indian War involved scouts and patrols, and did not result in any major engagements with hostile Indian forces. Fighting was typically limited to small-scale engagements. There were, however, an ample number of savage battles fought by these troops on the Texas frontier… and elsewhere. General Joseph J. Reynolds, commander of the fifth military district, expressed the sentiment of disappointment his troops felt chasing Indians over thousands of miles of rugged, dusty country and finding them nowhere…then everywhere. However frustrating, Reynolds emphasized that "all that is possible for their number to do has been done to protect the people and property of the frontier counties."[225]

One brutal encounter involved nine troopers of the 9th cavalry from Fort McKavett who were under the leadership of Sergeant Emanuel Stance. As cited earlier, on 20 May 1870, Sergeant Stance and his nine charges, commanded by Captain Henry Carroll, left the fort on routine patrol. They were searching for Indians who had stolen two children during a raid. Approximately fourteen miles from the post, near Kickapoo Creek, they observed a party of Indians escorting nine horses. The troopers attacked, and were engaged in a running fight for roughly eight miles when the Indians broke contact and abandoned the stolen animals. The soldiers camped overnight and headed back towards Fort McKavett the following morning with the captured horses. Along the way they encountered about twenty Indians who were stalking a herd of government horses and a small detachment of guards. Stance and the men attacked. The Indians retreated, but soon regrouped and mounted a counterattack. Stance and several of his men outflanked the attacking Indians, who broke from the engagement and fled. For his bravery under fire Sergeant Stance was awarded the Congressional Medal of Honor. Stance was the first black soldier who fought in the Indian War to receive this prestigious honor.[226]

---

[225] *Annual Report of the Secretary of War for the Year 1870.*
[226] William Carney was the first black soldier to receive the Congressional

Stance's record was later tarnished however. Sixteen years later, Stance, by then a First Sergeant, was still in the Army and was assigned to F Troop at Fort Robinson, Nebraska. Due to the somewhat boring duty, the non-commissioned officers of the unit began to lose control of their men. Stance was among the more rigid disciplinarians, and a center of the conflict. Residents of the guardhouse responded to the harsh discipline with violence. In December 1887, the body of First Sergeant Stance was found on the road to Crawford, Nebraska with four bullet wounds. Stance is believed to have been assassinated by his own troops.

In spring of 1873, companies of the 10th were transferred to Forts Richardson, Griffin and Concho. At various times, Buffalo Soldiers of the 9th and 10th Cavalry regiments served at virtually every Texas frontier fort from the Rio Grande to the Red River and on into the Panhandle. They participated in most of the major frontier campaigns of the period, and distinguished themselves in action against the Cheyenne, Kiowa, Comanche, Apache, Sioux, and Arapaho Indians. With outstanding officers such as Benjamin H. Grierson, Abner Doubleday, William Rufus Shafter, Joseph A. Mower and Edward Hatch, they were an important component of the frontier army. In total, black troops earned eighteen Congressional Medals of Honor during the Indian War campaigns.

Medal of Honor. He was awarded the distinguished medal for his actions on 18 July 1863 at Fort Wagner, South Carolina while a member of the 54th Massachusetts Regiment during the Civil War. The 54th was Massachusetts' first black regiment. During the calamitous battle at Ft. Wagner, Carney noticed that the man who carried the American flag had been wounded. He bravely rescued the banner and delivered it safely to his regiment, reportedly shouting, "Boys, the old flag never touched the ground." Carney was wounded during the battle. After the war he spent thirty-one years working for the US Postal Service. Finally, in May 1900, Carney became the first black to be awarded the Congressional Medal of Honor.

During the whole of the Indian Wars campaign, which lasted from about 1869 through 1881, there were 426 Congressional Medals of Honor awarded, 422 of which were earned by soldiers of the US Army and four by civilian scouts. Of the 426, black soldiers earned eighteen. Five of the eighteen were earned by black troopers during engagements in Texas.

In 1874 the government decided to take more decisive action against the Indians. Factors influencing that decision included an ever increasing hostile attitude on the part of the Indians, the stepped up raids, and two incidents in Texas known as the Second Battle of Adobe Walls and the Lost Valley fight. The campaign put an end to the long bloody war that had been waged on the West Texas Frontier. Subsequent to the resulting campaign, hostile Indians were placed on reservations across the west.

After the hostile Indian tribes had been displaced from West Texas, the Buffalo Soldiers were assigned to pursue them into New Mexico, Colorado and the Dakotas. After the Indian wars came to an end in the 1890s the four regiments continued in service, with elements participating in the Spanish-American War, the Philippine Insurrection, and John J. Pershing's 1916 punitive expedition.

In spite of the fact that most Buffalo Soldier units logged exemplary service, the records are dotted with incidents that detractors are quick to cite. In the middle of the summer of 1877, one of many drought years in West Texas, a troop of some forty Buffalo Soldiers struck out into the Llano Estacado from Double Lakes, south of modern Lubbock, in pursuit of a band of Kwahada Comanches who had been raiding homesteads and hunting parties. A group of twenty-two buffalo hunters accompanied the soldiers as guides and allies. Several days later three of the black troopers rode into Fort Concho and reported that the men and officers of Troop A were missing and presumed dead from thirst. The "Staked Plains Horror," as the incident was later dubbed, captured wide spread attention. Most of the soldiers eventually straggled back into camp. Four had died.[227] Four others eventually faced court-martial for desertion at Fort McKavett on 27 September 1877. The buffalo hunters had ridden off on their own to find water and left the black troops behind. The soldiers survived by drinking the blood of their dead horses and their own urine.

---

[227] Private John H. Bonds. "A" Company 10th Cavalry. Died 30 July 1877.
Private Isaac Derwin. "A" Company 10th Cavalry. Died 30 July 1877.
Private John Isaacs. "A" Company 10th Cavalry. Died 30 July 1877.
Private John T. Gordon. "A" Company 10th Cavalry. Died 30 July 1877.

What had begun as a routine army scout had turned into catastrophe. The deserters were found guilty, dishonorably discharged from the army, and locked up in a federal penitentiary.

The Buffalo Soldiers were not always welcomed into the communities near where they served. In one instance that occurred at San Angelo, Private Hiram Pinder of the Ninth Cavalry was shot and killed by a white gambler in a saloon. The townspeople helped the killer escape and he was never captured. Twelve days after Pinder's death, Private William Watkins was singing and dancing for drinks in another saloon. He tired of performing and decided to quit for the evening, but a rancher named Tom McCarthy insisted that he continue. When Watkins refused, McCarthy shot and killed him. McCarthy then fled, but he was captured by soldiers who turned him over to the sheriff. Instead of jailing McCarthy, however, the sheriff allowed him to remain free because killing a black person was only considered a minor crime. When he was finally tried for the murder of Private Watkins, an all-white jury found him not guilty.

Captain Richard Henry Pratt, 10th Cavalry Buffalo Soldiers, holds the distinction of being the officer who founded the Carlisle School for Indian Students. Pratt spent eight years (1867-1875) in Indian Territory as an officer of the 10th Cavalry, commanding a unit of Buffalo Soldiers and Indian Scouts. During this time, he was stationed at Ft. Sill, Oklahoma, sixty miles east of the site of the Battle of the Washita where Cheyenne Chief Black Kettle was killed in 1867. In 1875, Captain Pratt escorted seventy-two Indian warriors suspected of murdering white settlers to Fort Marion in St. Augustine, Florida. Once there, Pratt began an ambitious experiment that involved strict discipline and teaching the Indians to read and write English. Pratt made the wear military uniforms and drilling them like troops. His objective, as is characterized by his motto "Kill the Indian and save the man," meaning to force the Indians to give up their ancestral ways was not favorably viewed. Looking in retrospect, Indian tribes today find Pratt's actions to have been appalling.

At the time, however, Pratt's program met with popular acceptance. News of his experiment spread. With the blessing of congress, Pratt expanded the program by establishing the Carlisle School for Indian Students where he continued his mission to break their spirit and forever sever the children from their heritage by mandating cultural genocide.

The Carlisle schools continued into the 1930s until administrators saw that the promised result of transforming Indian students into "imitation white children" was an abject failure. Later, Indians who attended the schools told the awful story of an experiment gone horribly wrong, and how its consequences have been felt for generations of Indians.[228]

Buffalo Soldiers found themselves facing increasing racial prejudice at the turn of the century as well. They were often cut off from the segregated towns they were stationed near, and were the victims of slurs, beatings and harassment by law officers. As armed veterans of active service, they occasionally responded with violence. The Ninth Cavalry was involved in racial disturbances in Rio Grande City in 1899, the Twenty-fifth regiment allegedly attacked civilians in the Brownsville Raid of 1906, and the Twenty-fourth regiment was involved in the Houston Riot of 1917, also referred to as the Camp Logan Riot.

The Brownsville Affair was an incident that grew out of tensions between whites in Brownsville, Texas and black infantrymen stationed at nearby Fort Brown. The soldiers had not been treated well by locals since the time they had arrived. A shooting incident in town on the night of Monday, 13 August 1906 left a white bartender dead and a police officer wounded. Although white commanders at Fort Brown acknowledged that all black soldiers were in their barracks at the time of the shooting, local whites claimed that it was black soldiers who had been seen doing the shooting. The accusers produced spent cartridge cases from army rifles to support their claim. Despite evidence that indicated the shells had been planted, <u>investigators accepted the statements of the white community.</u>

---

[228] Pratt, Richard Henry.2004. *Battlefield and classroom : four decades with the American Indian, 1867-1904*. Norman, Oklahoma: University of Oklahoma Press. Also see - Eastman, Alaine Goodale. 1935. *Pratt, the Red Man's Moses*. Norman, Oklahoma: University of Oklahoma Press. Haley, James L.. 1976. *The Buffalo War: The History of the Red River Indian Uprising of 1874*. Garden City, New York: Doubleday.

When the black soldiers were pressured to name who had done the shooting they insisted that they had no knowledge of the incident. In spite of the fact that there was no trial, and the men were not given a hearing, President Theodore Roosevelt ordered that 167 black infantrymen be dishonorably discharged for their conspiracy of silence.

The Houston Riot of 1917, also referred to as the Camp Logan Riot, began on Thursday, 23 August 1917. Houston Police Officers E.G. Meinke, Ira Raney, Ross Patton, Horace Moody, and Rufus Daniels were all shot and killed during this race riots that was sparked by the arrest of several black soldiers assigned to Camp Logan. After an incident during which one soldier was arrested, and reportedly harassed by local citizens and law enforcement officers, a large mob of the soldiers stole rifles from the base and went on a rampage, shooting and killing a total of sixteen people throughout the city of Houston.

The violence that occurred during the night of Thursday 23 August 1917 is oftentimes referred to as the Camp Logan Riot, although the actions of the mutinous soldiers assigned to the camp took place away from the actual premises of the military base. Two locations were involved. First, along Buffalo Bayou in the suburban residential community of Brunner which is on the north side of Buffalo Bayou and at the intersection of Washington Avenue and the modern Shepherd Drive. The second riot scene was on the south side of Buffalo Bayou, along San Felipe Road (now known as West Dallas Avenue) in a residential area of the Fourth Ward known as the San Felipe District.

The events began when army Corporal Charles W. Baltimore, an off duty military policeman from the 3rd Battalion, was arrested and reportedly treated roughly by a Houston policeman. Rumors circulated that Baltimore had been killed, provoking anger and frustration among the troops. The disquiet continued to build during the early evening. To avoid an armed confrontation the commandant, Major Kneeland S. Snow, ordered all the rifles and ammunition collected. As the weapons were being gathered troops sighted a mob that was advancing toward the camp. Someone fired a shot, then chaos broke out. The soldiers raided the supply tent for their guns. They began firing indiscriminately into the residential neighborhood. A mob of over 100 soldiers poured out of the camp and on to the streets of the Brunner community, determined to march to the Fourth Ward jail and release their imprisoned comrade

Officers Rufus Daniel, W. C. Wilson, Horace Moody and C. E. Carter had commandeered a vehicle to ride to the action. They stopped the car stopped when they heard shots fired. Mob leader Sergeant Vida Henry ordered his men to take cover in the City Cemetery, located on the south side of the street. Officer Daniels unwisely decided to charge the troops in the cemetery armed only with his service revolver. He was instantly killed. Carter, Wilson and Moody took cover in a nearby garage. Moody was shot in the leg and severely injured. He later died while doctors were amputating his leg. The firing ceased, and the soldiers brutalized the corpse of Daniels, battering his face and bayoneting his body. Next the frenzied mob advanced toward downtown Houston.

At Heiner Street, four blocks into their route, the throng encountered a seven passenger touring car driven by James E. Lyon. The car had two civilian passengers along with police officers John E. Richardson and Ira Raney who had hitched a ride to get to the area where the violence was taking place. The mob disarmed the group in the vehicle and held them with their hands in the air. Richardson inadvertently let his hands down and was hit over the head with butt of a rifle by a soldier. At that point Officer Raney and the civilian passenger Eli Smith decided to take off running in hopes of reaching safety. Smith was shot. His body was later found in the ditch at Heiner Street. Smith had also been bayoneted in the hip and the left armpit. Officer Raney's was also shot. His body was beaten and bayoneted. Asa Bland, the other civilian passenger in the touring car, was shot as well. The bullet grazed him just over his left eye.

A second car arrived at the Heiner Street intersection. That vehicle carried Captain Joseph Mattes from Camp Logan, three enlisted soldiers and Police Officer Edwin Meinke. When Captain Mattes stood up in the car to address the out of control horde about forty of the soldiers took aim at the vehicle and opened fire. Both Mattes and Meinke were killed immediately.

During the melee detective T. A. Binford received a minor wound to the knee. In little more than two hours of violent rioting the mob had killed their own captain and five Houston police officers.

The now deflated mob retreated a few blocks to the south and re-formed ranks near the railroad tracks on the eastern edge of the Fourth Ward. By that time most of the soldiers had lost interest in their savage crusade and slowly drifted back to camp. No doubt fearing reprisal for his role in the affray, Sergeant Henry took his own life at about 2:05 a.m. the following morning.

On 24 August 1917, Governor James E. Ferguson declared martial law in Houston and placed Brigadier General John A. Hulen, commander of the Texas National Guard, in charge of the city. In an effort to restore order 350 Coast Guard servicemen were dispatched from Galveston, along with 600 infantrymen from San Antonio. By 9:30 a.m. on Saturday 25 August 1917, all of the troops of the 3rd Battalion had been loaded on trains and sent to either San Antonio or New Mexico to await trial. Order was restored to the city on Monday 27 August 1917.

A total of eleven citizens and five police officers were killed during this unspeakable disaster. Thirty citizens suffered severe wounds. Four of the rioting black soldiers were killed. Two fell at the hands of their own men, who mistook them for citizens. One soldier who had been shot by a citizen died in a hospital, and Sergeant Vida Henry died by his own hand.

Three separate courts martial were convened at Fort Sam Houston in San Antonio 1917. The magistrate indicted one hundred eighteen men of I Company, 24th Infantry, 3rd Battalion. Seven of the soldiers who rioted testified against the others in exchange for clemency. One hundred ten of the mutinous soldiers were found guilty of at least one charge. Nineteen of them were hanged, and sixty-three of them received life sentences. Two officers of Camp Logan faced courts martial, but were released.

But in spite of facing racial prejudice, and being at the center of ethnic ugliness like the Camp Logan affair, the Buffalo Soldiers left a positive and lasting imprint on the Texas Frontier and the American West. During the Indian Wars eighteen enlisted men from the black regiments earned the prestigious Congressional Medal of Honor. An additional five enlisted men (and one black sailor) won that decoration during the Spanish-American War. In total, however, there were 426 Congressional Medals of Honor awarded (422 of which were earned by soldiers of the US Army and four by civilian scouts).

None of the Buffalo Soldier regiments went to France during World War I. They did, however, provided a force of experienced noncommissioned officers to other black units that did go into combat. One black soldier, Corporal Freddie Stowers, did serve and receive the Congressional Medal of Honor. Stowers, of the 371st Infantry Regiment, 93rd Division, led his squad to destroy a group of enemy soldiers at Hill 188, Champagne, Marne Sector, France, and was leading them on to another trench when he was killed in action.

In the 1920s and 1930s, as black newspapers and civil-rights groups scrutinized the process, troops from the four black regiments were mainly used as laborers and service troops. The 9th and 10th cavalries were eventually disbanded, and their personnel transferred into other units during World War II. The 25th saw combat in the Pacific during the war, and was deactivated in 1949. The 24th also served in the Pacific during the Second World War, and fought in the opening stages of the Korean War. The Alaskan Highway was built by the all black 93rd, 95th, and 97th Engineering Regiments. The 24th, which was the last segregated black regiment to see combat, was deactivated in 1951, and its personnel were used to integrate other units serving in Korea at the time.[229]

Popular interest in the Buffalo Soldiers began to explode in the 1960s as broader interest in black history increased. Where once there was an information void, today there is no longer any shortage of books, scholarly papers, passionate articles, web-sites and other material devoted to the Buffalo Soldiers. In 1965 a reenactment unit, the 10th Cavalry Buffalo Soldiers, was formed. In the 1990s a reenactment group with the Texas Parks

---

[229] See - Ramos, Mary G. Ramos. *Texas Almanac 1990–1991*.
Also See - Carroll, John M. Carroll. 1971. *The Black Military Experience in the American West*. New York, New York: Liveright. Christian, Garna L.. 1995. *Black Soldiers in Jim Crow Texas, 1899–1917*. College Station, Texas: Texas A&M University Press. Leckie, William H.. 1967. *The Buffalo Soldiers: A Narrative of the Negro Cavalry in the West*. Norman, Oklahoma: University of Oklahoma Press.

and Wildlife Department offered a number of interpretive programs on the Buffalo Soldiers and performed at state parks and other venues. More recently, a Buffalo Soldiers National Museum has been established at Houston, Texas. This excellent facility offers and interpretive history of the troops as well as a display of artifacts of the period.

Although not welcomed by all, the Buffalo Soldiers left an indelible mark on the Texas landscape and were a significant factor in protecting settlers from Indian depredations during the post Civil War reconstruction era. It is rewarding to see that their service is finally being fully recognized.

"The Redoubtable Sergeant"
Image Courtesy of the Artist - Don Stivers @ Stivers Publishing

Chapter IX

STAGECOACH LINES, CATTLE TRAILS AND PEGLEG CROSSING

I cannot tell how the truth may be;
I say the tale as 'twas said to me.
Walter Scott

To violate the accepted convention of including some reference to stagecoaches, cattle trails and outlaws in any respectable book about the Old West would be nothing short of a sacrilege. Not wishing to contravene this custom, some mention of Pegleg Crossing and its associated malefactors, as well as the C. Bain & Company Stagecoach Line seems appropriate.

Pegleg Crossing on the San Saba River is an hourglass-shaped pass through the hills were McDougal Creek joins San Saba River. For years the spot was a preferred camping spot for Indians. In 1732 the spot was the site of an epic battle between Spanish Explorers and Apache Indians.

The Pegleg Crossing on the San Saba River was used almost continuously by the Spaniards from the time of the establishment of Santa Cruz de San Sabá in 1757 until the end of the colonial period. In 1849 William Henry Chase Whiting surveyed the portage as a part of a migration road to California. The crossing was a popular pathway for early adventurers, mustang hunters, Indian fighters, settlers, gold-seekers, stagecoach lines and cattle trails. Believed to have been named for the one-legged land commissioner T.W. Ward by landowner Wilhelm Harlen, the crossing served the army well, linking Fort

McKavett with San Antonio both before and after the Civil War. From 1867 until 1888 the San Antonio-San Diego (Southern Stage Line) used the military road. The stage line had a relay station, called Pegleg Station, constructed on a hill overlooking the ford.[230]

Pegleg gained notoriety for the numerous hold-ups that occurred there. In 1877 a group of highwaymen robbed the U.S. Mail at Pegleg Station, where the trail crosses the San Sabá River. Pegleg was a favorite locale for outlaws because of the favorable geography surrounding the crossing. The main trail that was used by stagecoaches crossed the San Sabá River at that point. Outlaws had a hideout called "the roost", or "robbers roost" nearby, from which they simply descended upon the passing stagecoaches, robbing the travelers and making off with the cargo. Robberies at this location were commonplace. In 1877 the robbery of the U.S. Mail at the Pegleg set into motion a series of events that led to a man hunt that lasted more than a year. The climax occurred when outlaw Dick Dublin, who along with his colleague in crime Ace Lankford who were wanted for murdering two men in Coryell County, were finally tracked down and killed by Texas Rangers on 18 January 1878.[231] It seems there was a $700 reward on the pair, providing further encouragement for lawmen.

Earlier attempts at the gang's capture had been embarrassing failures. Lieutenant Nelson Orcelus "N.O." Reynolds ordered a detachment of men to chase down Dublin and bring him to justice. In January 1878 a group of rangers including James Gillette, John and Will Bannister, Tom Gillespie, Dave Ligon and Ben Carter trailed the outlaws to Packsaddle Mountain near Junction City. They finally caught up with Dublin and his accomplices near the Potter Ranch on the South Llano River.[232] Alerted to the band of Rangers approaching, Dublin was shot in the back at a distance of 150 yards by Gillette. Gang menders

---

[230] Citing - Jimmy M. Skaggs, "PEGLEG CROSSING," *Handbook of Texas.* See - Hunter, J. Marvin Hunter. 1923. *Trail Drivers of Texas.* 2 vols.. San Antonio, Texas: Jackson Printing.
[231] Desmond, H.A. 1976. *Texas Knights of the Hill Country, Story of the Texas Rangers.* Bi-Centenial Edition 1976. Pages not numbered.
[232] Ibid.

swore revenge, but were unable to make good on their blood oath.

After a partner of the gang turned informer, Dick Dublin's brothers, Role and Dell, along with their companion hoodlum Mack Potter, and Reuben Boyce were captured and brought to justice.[233]

Three of the captured outlaws were convicted of the 1877 robbery of the U.S. Mail at Pegleg Station on 23-24 August 1880.

An interesting account of one traveler's experiences at Pegleg appeared in the *Galveston Daily News* of 12 April 1908:

> *After I returned from the Civil War I again returned to and followed my old trade for many years. Finally, I got the job of shoeing horses on the stage line from San Antonio to Fort Concho. I used to make regular trips over the line on stage. On one occasion, after returning from Fort Concho with the stage driver, John Chadwell, we were held up three miles from Menardville. It was a cold frosty night and we saw a bright blazing fire on the side of the road and men standing around it. We thought nothing of this until Winchesters were thrown upon us and we were ordered to get out and come to the fire to warm. The driver was also requested in a tone of one exercising authority to bring those sacks with brass locks. This John did without serious or stubborn protest. The sacks were ripped open and all their letters and packages were carefully searched for money and valuables under the glare of the blazing and crackling fire. After my first scare had passed and I felt that we would not be hurt, I remarked to John while gazing into the barrel of the Winchester, "Well, John this office of delivery has been established since we passed last." For this piece of pleasantry the robber who had me in charge gave me a jab on the head with his gun and replied, "Yes, we have established it for our special benefit and convenience, and you be careful how you use your tongue, or we will establish a graveyard in connection with it for you're sort." I needed no further invitation to hold my tongue, and I still carry a scar on my head as a relic of that night's experience. The next trip I made we were held up near*

---

[233] *Galveston Daily News.* 2 April 1880. Also see *Galveston Daily News.* 3 February 1882.

the same place. We were marched about 100 yards from the road into the chaparral and there the scoundrels broke our lamps and left us in the dark, and it was sleeting. Fortunately the driver, who was a cigarette smoker, had some matches and got a fire started, and we managed to take care of the ladies until morning, when we could see how to hitch up our team and continue our journey. The robbers knew us and I knew them and our turn came next to get even.

The stage owners furnished us, John Chadwell and myself with money and we stayed around Menardville two weeks or longer, drinking and playing billiards and carousing with the very men who had robbed us until we got them all located. Everything being ready and all the parties implicated in the robbery being properly located and identified, tried in U. S Court and convicted. One went to the penitentiary for 4 years and three went for 20 years each.

After the arrest, trial and conviction, it was not altogether safe and healthy for the witnesses and officers who had been connected with the prosecution of these robbers. The sheriff, while sitting in this house reading one night, received three loads of buckshot in his body. Two of the deputies or witnesses met death in a similar manner, and from the same source. Not knowing how soon Chadwell and myself would receive attention from the friends of these outlaws, I said to him that the climate of Menardville was not conductive to happiness, continued good health and long life, so far as we were concerned. And that we had better make ourselves scarce thereabouts, for awhile at least, and so we left. I do not know what became of John, but I went to San Antonio and remained there, until finally I decided to return to my home near Weimar.

The Western Cattle Trail made use of Pegleg Crossing. Serving as the primary thoroughfare for cattle drives heading to Kansas and beyond from nearby Kerrville and the Rio Grand Valley Pegleg Crossing was conveniently located along a natural path northward. Herds to be driven up the trail from the Mason area were assembled at Koocksville and were herded to meet the Western Trail which proceeded northward from Kerrville, crossing the Little Devils' River near the site of present

Noxville, the Llano River at Beef Trail Crossing, the San Saba at Pegleg Crossing, and Brady Creek west of Brady.

Numerous stagecoach lines operated in or through Menard County over the years, including the San Antonio-San Diego (Southern Stage Line), the San Antonio and El Paso, and C. Bain & Company Stagecoach Line.

Thomas Calvin Bain ran the stagecoach line known as the C. Bain & Company Stagecoach Line, serving the southwest part of Texas, including Mason, Menard, Fort Concho and San Antonio. Bain died in 1872, but the stage line continued to operate until as late as 1878.[234] Bain was born in Kentucky and came to Wood County in the 1850s where he married Samantha Angeline Waskom in 1865.

The once visible remains of the historic sites where the old Splittgerber Stage Stand once stood along on the Fort McKavett highway (State Highway 190) about six and one-half miles west of Menard are no more. Highway construction decades ago all but obliterated the site, which now can only be located by a handful of the most experienced and knowledgeable local historians. Benjamin and Slaughter Ficklan constructed the stage stop in the fall and winter of 1869-1870. The stop is located on the route between San Antonio and El Paso. Now little more than crumbling ruins, it remains as a reminder to passersby that travel was once far more time consuming, difficult, inconvenient and dangerous.[235] The old stage stand's proprietor, Oscar Otto Splittgerber was born 19 July 1836 in Germany. He reportedly came to America at the age of eighteen, and married Martha Shellenberger-Kingston around 1860. Some sources claim that Splittgerber went to Mexico 1860s. He had returned by 1870 however, because he appears on the Menard County census for that year. Also noted are his wife Martha, a seven year old named Fannie and his eleven year old stepson William Kingston. Oscar and Martha had three children in all. He died on 15 November 1890, and is buried in the Splittgerber/Ellis Cemetery in Menard County.

---

[234] Wood County Historical Society. 1976. *Wood County, 1850-1900*. Denton, Texas: University of North Texas.
[235] *Menard News and Messenger.* 18 June 1936.

Splittgerber Stage Stand
Old Splittgerber Stage Stand
Courtesy of Menard County Historical Museum

Cowboy Bathtub
Author's Collection

Not far from the site of the Splittgerber Stage Stand is a spot along the San Saba River referred to locally by some as the "cowboy bathtub." Others simply call it the whirlpool. In any case, as legend has it trail weary cowboys would stop at this spot along the trail between Menardville and Fort McKavett to enjoy an invigorating bath in the whirlpool of a naturally formed rock bathtub in the river. The site is still used by locals for a similar purpose, however the author has it on good authority that in lieu of being an ideal site for ones ablution it is a comforting spot to enjoy a cool adult beverage on a hot summer day.

The topic of stagecoach lines in Texas is a perplexing one. Period, as well as contemporary accounts are riddled with contrariety regarding which lines served what towns, and when and how effectively they operated. At least one respected Texas historian is claimed to be shouldering the daunting task of sorting this mess out. Hopefully a more accurate and well researched thesis, or book, will be forthcoming. In the mean time, readers are left to a variety of sometimes questionable sources. None-the-less, Rex H. Stever's synopsis of stage lines, which can be found on the Texas State Historical Association's *Handbook of Texas,* provides a well grounded primer which has been cited extensively throughout this chapter.

Contrary to how stage lines have been portrayed by Hollywood motion picture producers, the fact is that stage line operations were generally closely tied to government mail contracts. These contracts provided the stage line operators with a solid financial footing upon which their companies could also transport passengers and freight. The stagecoach routes themselves provided a network of well traveled pathways by which mail delivery was made possible to all communities.

Texas postal routes were first established by the Texas Provisional Government in the fall of 1835. Originally only fifteen routes were set up, serving the more populated communities in the central, southern, and eastern portions of the Republic. Individuals on horseback provided service to many of the early communities. Most of the early stage lines were short. By May 1839 a route was operating between the burgeoning community of Houston and Washington-on-the-Brazos.[236] Later that year a line from Houston to Egypt, via Richmond, and a line between Houston and Austin began running.

---

[236] Washington-on-the-Brazos, site of the birthplace of the Texas Republic, is located on the Brazos River, on FM 1155, southwest of Navasota.

In late 1845 the firm of Brown and Tarbox, which was likely the principal line of the day, operated a biweekly service by the Houston and Austin Mail Stage Line via Washington, Independence, La Grange, and Bastrop.[237] By 1847 its "Texas United States Mail Line" was providing biweekly service between Houston and San Antonio, and its Western United States Mail Line furnished biweekly service between Port Lavaca and San Antonio. Also in 1847, John Sutherland began a weekly stage run from Houston to Victoria via Richmond, Egypt, and Texana.

The rapidly growing inland areas of Texas needed a connection to the Gulf Coast ports, where supplies and settlers were arriving. By 1848 bimonthly service between San Antonio and Corpus Christi had commenced. In December 1849 the firm of Harrison and Brown began weekly service between San Antonio and Lavaca via Seguin, Gonzales, Cuero, and Victoria. In 1851 James L. Allen ran a stage between San Antonio and Indianola by a similar route, with an extra stop at New Braunfels.

The mental image of smartly dressed men and women bouncing along peacefully in a stagecoach traveling through a pastoral setting, piloted by a rugged looking and bearded driver and a fierce appearing fellow wearing a lawman's badge riding shotgun is pure motion picture fiction. Stagecoach travel was dangerous, dirty and tiresome. It was wrought with peril from bandits as well as hostile Indians. This was especially the case in the interior of Texas, for communities like San Antonio, Austin, and the emerging Hill Country region to the west. Stage owners regularly reported thefts of mules and supplies. Way stations were raided and destroyed. Indians murdered drivers, guards and passengers. In spite of the threat, new stage lines were added yearly as the population grew and expanded westward.

Stage service to the western reaches of the state was brought about, in large part, by the California gold rush. Henry Skillman was granted a contract to provide mail service from San Antonio to Santa Fe, via El Paso, and launched that enterprise on 20 September 1851. The first San Antonio-El Paso Mail stage departed the Alamo City on 3 November 1851. But in

[237] Citing Rex H. Stever. *Handbook of Texas.*

April 1854 Skillman's contract was revoked, and a new one awarded to David Wasson. Wasson, however, failed to deliver and the contract was transferred to George H. Giddings that same year.

Giddings and Skillman suffered heavy financial losses from Indian raids, lost mail, destroyed stations, the murder of station hands, stage guards, drivers, and passengers. None-the-less, they won increased compensation from the U.S. Post Office Department. The company was still operating when, on 22 June 1857, a contract was granted to James Birch for service from San Antonio to San Diego, California, via El Paso. Birch's triumph was short lived. After his death Giddings bought the contract, and continued service until the El Paso to Fort Yuma portion of the covenant was terminated in October 1858.

One of the most famous and romantically popularized stagecoach operations in Texas was the Butterfield Overland Mail. One can practically hear the crack of the bullwhip urging the four or six horse (or mule) hitch onward as the Butterfield prairie schooner cruised almost effortlessly through the cactus and mesquite dotted grasslands of Texas.

Californians demanded faster mail service from the east, namely an overland stage route to the West Coast. As a result, on 2 July 1857, a contract was awarded to John Butterfield of Utica, New York, who had agreed to run a southern route through El Paso. Butterfield's path was favored by Postmaster General Brown because it could provide year-round service, whereas the mid-continent and northern routes had to be shut down in winter months due to heavy snows in the mountain passes.

Although some dispute exists, Butterfield's stage route is fairly well documented. The path headed southwest from St. Louis and Memphis, crossing the Red River at Colbert's Ferry in Grayson County and continuing across Texas for 282 miles to Fort Chadbourne via Jacksboro, Fort Belknap, and Fort Phantom Hill. The next 458 miles to El Paso swung south across a barren plain between the Concho and Pecos rivers, past Horsehead Crossing where water was in short supply, then up the east bank to Pope's Camp where the trail crossed the river, hugged the west bank northwestward to Delaware Spring, and then turned westward through Guadalupe Pass to Hueco Tanks and El Paso.[238] The line continued westward, through Tucson and Fort Yuma to San Diego. To service the teams and passengers, the company built stations every twenty miles along the route and drilled water wells where no live water was available. Relief mules were kept at the stations, but they were often stolen or driven off by Indians.[239] The first Butterfield stages began the eastbound run on 15 September 1858. The westbound began on 16 September 1858.

At the beginning of the Civil War the United States Congress passed legislation that transferred the Butterfield line from Texas to a more northern route. The Confederates seized all the Butterfield stations and many of the company's coaches, thus ending this epic saga in Texas stage lines history.

At the onset of the Civil War there had been about thirty-one stage lines operating in the Lone Star State. Some of these lines continued to operate after the war began, and mail lines carried on out of San Antonio and other important Texas communities. Confederate wagons, loaded to beyond capacity, creaked as teams of oxen strained while plodding their way down the "Cotton Road" between Brownsville-Matamoros and the railhead at Alleyton.[240] Many of the teamsters were men who were too old to serve in the army, or boys who were too young. Some were conscripted, and forced to take loads of cotton to Brownsville, for which they were paid $10 a month in

---

[238] Ibid.

[239] Quoting Rex H. Stever. *Handbook of Texas*. Also see - Wayne R. Austerman, *Sharps Rifles and Spanish Mules: The San Antonio-El Paso Mail, 1851–1881* (College Station: Texas A&M University Press, 1985).

ter Braake, Alex L. 1970. *Texas: The Drama of Its Postal Past*. Fredericksburg, Maryland: American Philatelic Society. Konwiser, Harry M. 1933. *Texas Republic Postal System*. New York, New York: Lindquist. Ormsby, Waterman L. 1955. *The Butterfield Overland Mail*. San Marino, California: Huntington Library. Thornhoff, Robert H. 1971. *San Antonio Stage Lines, 1847–1881*. El Paso, Texas: Texas Western Press

[240] The Cotton Road began at Alleyton, near present day Columbus, which was the terminus of the railroad from Houston. The road ended at the Rio Grande, at the extreme end of the Confederate controlled territory. The Cotton Road ran ten miles west of Corpus Christi, along the old Matamoros Road. The cotton came down in a never-ending stream, with hundreds of wagons hauling thousands of bales, bringing gold and wartime materiel on the return leg of the haul.

Confederate currency. Each drove a wagon pulled by four yoke of oxen. *Los Algodones,* the cotton times, was a boom era for Mexico as well as Texas cotton producers. From Matamoros, cotton was hauled twenty-five miles east to the fishing village of Bagdad, a simple shantytown filled with tent hotels and open air restaurants. The arriving cotton was piled everywhere, waiting to be loaded onto ships moored at the mouth of the Rio Grande. By some accounts as many as 300 vessels rested at anchor awaiting their cargoes of cotton.

In the years after the Civil War hundreds of United States mail contracts covering Texas routes were awarded. Many were for short routes between small towns, resulting in stage service to nearly every community in the Lone Star State. In April 1866 Bethel Coopwood began service between San Antonio and El Paso, but control of the line passed to Benjamin F. Ficklin in 1867. After Ficklin's death in March 1871 the contract for this service was awarded to his partner, F. P. Sawyer of Washington, D.C. Sawyer operated the line through June 1875. Although the coming of the railroad signaled the end of the stagecoach era, some stage lines continued to operate from the railheads into the more remote frontier areas. Among the last was the earlier cited C. Bain and Company. Charles Bain's company operated from early 1876 into the 1880s with a route from San Antonio to Fort Concho, connecting with another Bain line from Ben Ficklin to El Paso and Mesilla, New Mexico. Bain also operated stages between San Antonio and Laredo.

By the early 1880s the stagecoach era was essentially over, supplanted by more cost effective service by railroad. In rural areas, however, some stage service survived into the next century. Much like the short-lived age of the cowboy, the striking image of a majestic stagecoach and a young boy or girl's dream of travel beyond their small rural realm, had vanished forever. The factories of companies like Abbot & Downing of Concord, New Hampshire and M. P. Henderson; Stockton, California who made the rugged schooners of the plains soon ceased production. Another icon had passed into history.

EPILOGUE

I will a round unvarnish'd tale deliver.
William Shakespear

    Epilogues are not epitaphs, but the death knell has long since sounded for the traditional American Cowboy and the rugged, yet hopeful and resistant lifestyle of the early Texas pioneer. Collectively, history aficionados have a decided bias towards romanticizing the era of the Old West. Perhaps to some it represents a time and place where a man's word was his bond, and honesty was not just practiced when someone was looking. It was a time when one's good name meant something. Men tipped their hats to ladies, opened doors and conversed politely, with respect. Not all women were ladies, and ladies dressed like ladies and everyone knew the difference. It was an era when Americans seemed more hopeful. Success was just there, at the tip of ones fingers. Hard work, not so much cleverness and scheming, still led to prosperity. It was a time when folks proudly flew the American Flag, and public prayer was still okay.

    Lawmen, although they were rawhide tough head knockers, were generally respected members of the community who knew how to keep the peace, not simply enforce the law. Not wishing to sound disrespectful, but looking back, those brave marshals, constables, sheriffs, deputies and Texas Rangers seem to stand in stark contrast to the largely youthful, shaved headed crowd of today whose appearance is often more reminiscent of someone out of a science fiction movie than the quintessential image a tough old law dog with a Stetson pulled down over his eyes and a big Colt .45 strapped to his hip.

    On the other hand, let's not forget that life could be positively toilsome at time. Bathrooms were outdoors, if there was one. There was no air conditioning, television, electricity, telephones, or any of the associated modern convenience that we all seem to rely on today. The fire ants had not yet arrived, but the chiggers, ticks and scorpions were abundant. Some wise person once said that life in Texas was "heaven for men and dogs, and hell for women and oxen." To go along with that adage it was no joke that "everything in Texas will stick you or bite you."

On balance, however, our silent thoughts tend to treat the bygone era kindly, perhaps longing for simpler times. The windswept prairies and rugged Hill Country saw the coming and going of the Indians, Spanish explorers, Mexican impresarios, and a succession of governance. The land that once was used for hunting and fishing became the dinner plate for millions of cattle, sheep and goats. Cotton supplanted much of the livestock ranching, followed by the oil boom and the oil bust. Now tourism and wildlife enterprises have replaced, or augmented, much of the ranching. The burden of taxation and the ever-increasing cost of fuel, supplies, feed has caused many fifth and sixth generation Texas ranchers to throw in the towel, sell off the home place, and move to town. Young folks starting out today in agricultural enterprises face a daunting challenge. None-the-less, these loyal and resolute sons and daughters of Texas are soldiering on ...regardless. Such folks as this make their homes, and thrive, at Fort McKavett and in Menard County. Their story is an admirable one. I hope you enjoyed it.

APPENDIX A

Pre Civil War Soldiers who died while at Fort McKavett.[241]

Date	Name	Rank & Regiment
3/31/52	Christian Weaver	PVT 8th Inf.
8/26/52	Francis Christopher	8th Inf.
9/13/52	Washington P. Street	1st Lt. 8th Inf.
12/2/52	John Palmer	PVT 8th Inf.
1/21/53	David McKee	PVT 8th Inf.
1/22/53	Patrick Fitzsimmons	PVT 8th Inf.
3/1/53	James Willet	PVT 8th Inf.
4/26/53	Ernst Klinger	Recruit Unassigned
7/4/53	William Morris	PVT 8th Inf.
10/6/53	George McCabe	PVT 1st Inf.
10/10/53	Henry Collin	PVT 8th Inf.
7/31/55	Jakob Wolf	PVT 2nd Dragoons
8/4/55	Edward Burne	PVT 1st Inf.
8/30/55	Albert Eppler	PVT 1st Inf.
10/7/55	John Cotter	PVT 1st Inf.
10/26/55	John D. McCall	2nd Lt. 1st Inf.
1/23/56	Richard Young	PVT 1st Inf.
4/26/56	Louis Bauer	PVT 1st Inf.
7/27/56	Peter Thornton	PVT 1st Inf.
1/27/57	Daniel Herne	PVT 1st Inf.
1/12/58	Myron H. Clark,	PVT 1st Inf.
12/31/58	Michael Meagher	PVT 1st Inf.

---

[241] *Fort McKavett Gazette*. Volume 2 Number 3. March 2003.

Bibliography

Books & Scholarly Works

- Alexander, Bob. 2007. *Lawmen, Outlaws and S.O.B.'s, Volume II: Gunfigthers of the Old West.* Silver City, New Mexico: High-Lonesome Books.
- Arnold, James R. 2000. *Jeff Davis's Own: Cavalry, Comanches, and the Battle for the Texas Frontier.* New York, New York: John Wiley & Sons, Inc.
- Austerman, Wayne . 1985. *Sharps Rifles and Spanish Mules: The San Antonio-El Paso Mail, 1851-1881.* . College Station, Texas: Texas A&M University Press.
- Barrett, Arrie. 1927. *Federal Military Outposts in Texas.* M.A. Thesis. University of Texas.
- Berlandier, Jean Louis. 1990. *Indians of Texas in 1830.*
- Biesele, Rudolph L. 1964. *The History of the German Settlements in Texas, 1831–1861.* Austin, Texas: Von Boeckmann-Jones.
- Bolton, Herbert Eugene. 1915. *Texas in the Middle Eighteenth Century: Studies in Spanish Colonial History and Administration.* Berkeley, California: University of California Press.
- Brown, John Henry. 1970. *History of Texas 1685 to 1892.* Austin, Texas: Pemberton Press.
- Caldwell, Clifford R. and DeLord, Ron. 2011. *Texas Lawmen 1835-1899, The Good and the Bad.* Charleston, South Carolina: The History Press.
- Caldwell, Clifford R. 2010. *A Day's Ride From Here, Volume I – Mountain Home, Texas.* Charleston, South Caroline. The History Press.
- Carroll, John M. Carroll. 1971. *The Black Military Experience in the American West.* New York, New York: Liveright.
- Centennial Committee Harper, Texas. 1963. *Here's Harper.* Fredericksburg, Texas: Dietel & Son.
- Christian, Garna L. 1995. *Black Soldiers in Jim Crow Texas, 1899–1917.* College Station, Texas: Texas A&M University Press.

- Cochran, Keith. 1992. *American West – A Historical Chronology*. Rapid City, South Dakota.
- Cochran, Keith. 1994. *Colt Peacemaker Collector – Pocket Compendium*. Rapid City, South Dakota.
- Crimmins, M. L. "W. G. Freeman's Report on the Eighth Military Department," *Southwestern Historical Quarterly*. Volume 51-54. July 1947-October 1950.
- DeArment, Bob. "The Killing of John W. Vaden by a Man Named Ben Daniels," *Wild West History Journal*. Volume 1. Number 1. February 2008.
- Desmond, H.A. 1976. *My Search for Las Almagres Mine, Later Called Bowie's Mine*. Bi-Centenial Edition 1976.
- Desmond, H.A. 1976. *Texas Knights of the Hill Country, Story of the Texas Rangers*. Bi-Centenial Edition 1976.
- Dickson, Lucy Lee. 1941. "Speculation of John Charles Beales in Texas Lands." M.A. thesis. University of Texas.
- Dobak, William A. and Phillips, Thomas D. 2001. *Black Regulars, 1866-1898*. Norman, Oklahoma: University of Oklahoma Press.
- Eastman, Alaine Goodale. 1935. *Pratt, the Red Man's Moses*. Norman, Oklahoma: University of Oklahoma Press.
- Eilers, Kathryn Burford. 1939. *A History of Mason County, Texas*. M.A. thesis. University of Texas.
- Estep, Raymond."The First Panhandle Land Grant." *Chronicles of Oklahoma* 36. Winter 1958–59.
- Everett, Dianna. 1990. *The Texas Cherokees: A People between Two Fires, 1819–1840*. Norman, Oklahoma: University of Oklahoma Press.
- Ewers, John C. (Editor). Translated by Patricia Reading Leclerq. 1969. *The Indians of Texas in 1830 by Jean Louis Berlandier*. Washington, D.C: Smithsonian Institution Press.
- Fehrenbach, T.R. 1968. *Lone Star: A History of Texas and the Texans*. New York, New York: Collier Books.
- Fehrenbach, T.R. 1979. *Comanches: The Destruction of a People*. New York, New York: Alfred A. Knopf.
- Fisher, O.C. 1937. *It Occurred In Kimble*. Houston, Texas: Jones Press.

- Fowler, Arlen. 1971. *The Black Infantry in the West, 1869-1891*. Westport, Connecticut: Greenwood Publishing Group, Inc.
- Frazer, Robert W. Frazer. 1965. *Forts of the West*. Norman, Oklahoma: University of Oklahoma Press.
- Gillett, James B.. 1921. *Six Years with the Texas Rangers, 1875-1881*. Austin, Texas: Von Boeckmann-Jones.
- Haley, J. Evetts. 1952. *Fort Concho and the Texas Frontier*. San Angelo, Texas: San Angelo Standard-Times.
- Haley, James L. 1976. *The Buffalo War: The History of the Red River Indian Uprising of 1874*. Garden City, New York: Doubleday.
- Hart, Herbert M. 1980. *Tour Guide to Old Western Forts*. Boulder, Colorado: Pruett.
- Henderson, Mary Virginia."Minor Empresario Contracts for the Colonization of Texas, 1825–1834," *Southwestern Historical* Hill, Joseph John. 1921. *The Old Spanish Trail*. Baltimore, Maryland: Williams and Wilkins.
- Holden, William Curry. 1928. *Frontier Problems and Movements in West Texas*. Ph.D. Dissertation. University of Texas.
- Hood, John Bell.1880. *Advance and Retreat: Personal Experiences in the United States and Confederate States Armies*. New Orleans, Louisiana: Beauregard.
- Hunter, Marvin J. 1920. *Trail Drivers of Texas*. 2 Volumes. San Antonio, Texas: Jackson Printing.
- Hunter, J. Marvin. "Fort McKavett Has Interesting Early History.' *Frontier Times*. Volume 8, Number 2. November 1930.
- Ivey, Darren L. 1970. *The Texas Rangers, A Registry and History*. Jefferson, North Carolina. McFarland & Company.
- Jinks, Roy. 1977. *History of Smith & Wesson*. North Hollywood, California: Beinfeld Publishing.
- John, Elizabeth A. H.. 1975. *Storms Brewed in Other Men's Worlds: The Confrontation of Indians, Spanish, and French in the Southwest, 1540–1795*. College Station, Texas: Texas A&M University Press.

- Jordan, Terry G. 1966. *German Seed in Texas Soil: Immigrant Farmers in Nineteenth-Century Texas.* Austin, Texas: University of Texas Press.
- King, Grace and McGuigan, Sherwood Noel and Mecham, Gem. 1992. *From Muskets to Mohair, The History of Fort Terrett.* Waco, Texas: Texian Press.
- Konwiser, Harry M. 1933. *Texas Republic Postal System.* New York, New York: Lindquist.
- Kopec, John A. 1985. *A Study of the Colt Single Action Army Revolver.* Dallas, Texas: Taylor Publishing.
- La Vere, David. 2004. *The Texas Indians.* College Station, Texas: Texas A&M.
- Lee, Jr., R. E. 1904. *Recollections and Letters of General Robert E. Lee.* New York, New York: Doubleday.
- Leckie, William H. 1967. *The Buffalo Soldiers: A Narrative of the Negro Cavalry in the West.* Norman, Oklahoma: University of Oklahoma Press.
- Loving, Solon Ollie. "A History of the Fisher-Miller Land Grant from 1842–1860" M.A. thesis. University of Texas. 1934.
- Mackay, Angus .1977. *Spain in the Middle Ages: From Frontier to Empire, 1000-1500.* New York, New York: St. Martin's Press.
- Madis, George. 1981. *The Winchester Book.* Ann Arbor, Michigan: Edwards Bros.
- McConnell, Joseph Carroll. 1933. *West Texas Frontier.* Vol. 1. Jacksboro, Texas: Vertical Files. Barker Texas History Center. University of Texas at Austin.
- McHenry, Roy C. and Roper, Walter F.. *1994. Smith & Wesson Hand Guns.* Prescott, Arizona: Wolfe Publishing.
- Menard County Historical Society. 1982. *Menard County History-An Anthology.* San Angelo, Texas: Anchor.
- Miller, Ray. 1985. *Ray Miller's Texas Forts.* Houston, Texas: Cordovan.
- Moore, Stephen L. 2010. *Savage Frontier Volume IV, Rangers, Riflemen and Indian Wars in Texas.* Denton, Texas: University of North Texas Press.

- Newcomb, William W. 1961. *The Indians of Texas.* Austin, Texas: University of Texas Press.
- Oommen, Sheena. *"Hin' nach Texas!* - Off to Texas!" Unpublished Manuscript. Undated.
- Ormsby, Waterman L. 1955. *The Butterfield Overland Mail.* San Marino, California: Huntington Library.
- Pierce, Michael D. 1993. *The Most Promising Young Officer: A Life of Ranald Slidell Mackenzie.* Norman, Oklahoma: University of Oklahoma Press.
- Pirkle, Arthur. 2002. *Winchester Lever Action Repeating Firearms – The Model 1866, 1873 & 1876 - Volume I.* Tustin, California: North Cape Publishing.
- Pratt, Richard Henry. 2004. *Battlefield and classroom : four decades with the American Indian, 1867-1904.* Norman, Oklahoma: University of Oklahoma Press.
- Rister, Carl Coke. 1946. *Robert E. Lee in Texas.* Norman, Oklahoma: University of Oklahoma Press.
- Rister, Carl Coke. 1955. *Comanche Bondage: Dr. John Charles Beales's Settlement of La Villa de Dolores on Las Moras Creek in Southern Texas of the 1830s.* Glendale, California: Clark.
- Robinson III, Charles M. 1993. *Bad Hand, A Biography of General Ranald Slidell Mackenzie.* State House Press.
- Rudolph L. Biesele. 1964. *The History of the German Settlements in Texas, 1831–1861.* Austin, Texas: Von Boeckmann-Jones. 1964).
- Schubert, Frank N. 1997. *Black Valor, Buffalo Soldiers and the Medal of Honor 1870-1898.* Lanham, Maryland: Rowman & Littlefield Publishers, Inc.
- Simpson, Harold B. 1979. *Cry Comanche: The Second U.S. Cavalry in Texas.* Hillsboro, Texas: Hill Junior College Press.
- Smith, David Paul. 1992. *Frontier Defense in the Civil War: Texas' Rangers and Rebels.* College Station, Texas: Texas A&M University Press.
- Smith, Thomas T. 1999. *The U.S. Army and the Texas Frontier Economy, 1845-1900.* College Station, Texas: Texas A&M University Press.

- Smith, Thomas T. 2000. *The Old Army in Texas: A Research Guide to the U.S. Army in Nineteenth-Century Texas*. Austin, Texas: Texas State Historical Association.
- Sullivan, Jerry M. 1981. *Fort McKavett, A Texas Frontier Post*. Lubbock, Texas: Texas Parks and Wildlife.
- Supica, Jim and Nahas, Richard. 2006. *Standard Catalog of the Smith & Wesson*. Gun Digest Books.
- ter Braake, Alex L. 1970. *Texas: The Drama of Its Postal Past*. Fredericksburg, Maryland: American Philatelic Society.
- Thornhoff, Robert H. 1971. *San Antonio Stage Lines, 1847–1881*. El Paso, Texas: Texas Western Press.
- Traverse, James Wadsworth. 1929. *From Coast to Coast via the Old Spanish Trail*. San Diego, California.
- Utley, Robert M. 1967. *Frontiersmen in Blue: The United States Army and the Indian, 1848-1865*. McMillan, New York: University of Nebraska Press.
- Utley, Robert M. 1973. *Frontier Regulars: The United States Army and the Indian, 1865-1891*. McMillan, New York: University of Nebraska Press.
- Wallace, Ernest and E. Adamson Hoebel. 1952. *The Comanches: Lords of the South Plains*. Norman, Oklahoma: University of Oklahoma Press.
- Warren, John. "The Vengeance of "Humpy" Jackson." *Frontier Times*. Volume 4 Number 11. August 1927.
- Webb, Walter Prescott. 2003. *The Texas Rangers, A Century of Frontier Defense*. Austin, Texas: University of Texas Press.
- Weddle, Robert S. 1964. *The San Saba Mission*. Austin, Texas: University of Texas Press.
- Whiting, William Henry Chase. 1938. "Journal of William Henry Chase Whiting." *Exploring Southwest Trails*. Volume 7 of *Southwest Historical Series*. Edited by Ralph P. Bieber and Leroy C. Hafen. Glendale, California: Arthur C. Clarke.
- Wilbarger, J.W. 1985. *Indian Depredations in Texas*. Austin, Texas: State House Press.
- Winslow, Edith Black. 1950. *In Those Days: Memories of the Edwards Plateau*. San Antonio, Texas: Naylor.

- Wiley Crimmins, M. L. "The First Line of Army Posts Established in West Texas in 1849." *West Texas Historical Association Year Book 19.* 1943.
- Wilkerson, Don. 1998. *Colt's Double Action Revolver Model 1878.* Marceline, Missouri: Wadsworth Publishing.
- Weaver, Bobby D. 1985. *Castro's Colony: Empresario Development in Texas, 1842-1865.* College Station, Texas: Texas A&M University Press.
- Weaver, John Downing. 1997. *The Senator and the Sharecropper's Son.* College Station, Texas: Texas A&M University Press.
- Webb, Walter Prescott. 2003. *The Texas Rangers, A Century of Frontier Defense.* Austin, Texas: University of Texas Press.
- Weddle, Robert S. 1964. *The San Saba Mission, Spanish Pivot in Texas.* Austin, Texas: University of Texas Press.
- Weddle, Robert S. 2000. *The San Sabá Papers.* Dallas, Texas: Southern Methodist University Press.
- Whiting, William Henry Chase. 1938. "Journal of William Henry Chase Whiting." *Exploring Southwest Trails.* Volume 7 of *Southwest Historical Series.* Edited by Ralph P. Bieber and Leroy C. Hafen. Glendale, California: Arthur C. Clarke.
- Winslow, Edith Black. 1950. *In Those Days: Memories of the Edwards Plateau.* San Antonio, Texas: Naylor.
- Wood County Historical Society. 1976. *Wood County, 1850-1900.* Denton, Texas: University of North Texas.
- Wyatt, Frederica Burt. "A Bad Time in Kimble County". *The Junction Eagle, Hunters & Visitors Guide 2002.* Wednesday, 30 October 2002.
- Yoakum, Henderson K. 2010. *History of Texas: from its first settlement in 1685 to its annexation to the United States in 1846.* Nabu Press.

Newspapers & Articles
- *Austin Daily Statesman.* 13 August 1886
- *Dallas Morning News.* 27 February 1886
- *Dallas Morning News.* 2 March 1886

- *Dallas Morning News.* 4 March 1886
- *Dallas Morning News.* 9 August 1886
- *Dallas Morning News.* 15 September 1886
- *Fort McKavett Gazette.* Volume 1 Number 6. November 2002
- *Fort McKavett Gazette.* Volume 2 Number 2. February 2003
- *Fort McKavett Gazette.* Volume 2 Number 3. March 2003
- *Fort McKavett Gazette.* Volume 3 Number 6. June 2004.
- *Fort McKavett Gazette.* Volume 4 Number 6. June 2005
- *Fort McKavett Gazette.* Volume 5 Number 3. March 2006
- *Fort McKavett Gazette.* Volume 5 Number 9. September 2006
- *Fort McKavett Gazette.* Volume 6 Number 1. January 2007
- *Fort McKavett Gazette.* Volume 9 Number 1. January 2010
- *Fort McKavett Gazette.* Volume 9 Number 5. May 2010
- *Fort Worth Gazette.* 7 August 1886
- *Galveston Daily News. 13 August 1868*
- *Galveston Daily News. 22 March 1870*
- *Galveston Daily News. 27 August 1870*
- *Galveston Daily News. 15 April 1871*
- *Galveston Daily News. 6 August 1873*
- *Galveston Daily News. 20 November 1873*
- *Galveston Daily News. 30 April 1874*
- *Galveston Daily News. 5 June 1875*
- *Galveston Daily News.* 30 November 1878
- *Galveston Daily News.* 2 April 1880
- *Galveston Daily News.* 3 February 1882
- *The Menard Messenger.* Volume 10. Number 48. Thursday, 11 October 1917
- *Menard News.* 9 March 1939

Other

- *Annual Report of the Secretary of War for the Year 1870.*
- General Order 95. Eighth Military District, 16 December 1851. RG 94. National Archives.
- General Order 11. Eighth Military District. 16 February 1852. RG 94. National Archives.

- The Haley Memorial Library and History Center at Midland, Texas, Director J. P. "Pat" McDaniel and staff.
- Menard County Land Deed Records. Menard County, Texas. Volume I, pp 129-199. *Abstract of All Original Texas Land Titles.* 8 Volumes.
- Mobley, Cody. Manuscript on the Role of Fort McKavett during the American Civil War. Copy dated 27 September 2011.
- National Archives and Records Administration (NARA). Washington, D.C.. Letter from First Lieutenant George E. Albee to Second Lieutenant Eugene D. Dimmick, acting post adjutant. Fort Concho, Texas. 1 July 1869.
- National Archives and Records Administration (NARA). Washington, D.C. Sections III and IV of Special Order No. 67. Fort McKavett, Texas. 9 June 1870.
- National Archives and Records Administration (NARA). Washington, D.C.. Report of Colonel MacKenzie. 3 February 1870. Concerning the capture of John "Humpy" Jackson and the murder of two soldiers.
- National Archives and Records Administration (NARA). Washington, D.C.. Letter of Colonel MacKenzie. 15 February 1870. Transmitting affidavit to Colonel Woods.
- National Archives and Records Administration (NARA). Washington, D.C. First Lieutenant George E. Albee's report to Captain Gamble at Fort Concho. 17 June 1869.
- National Archives and Records Administration (NARA). Washington, D.C. Letter of Colonel MacKenzie to Judge David Sheeks. 13 April 1870.
- National Archives and Records Administration (NARA). Washington, D.C. Captain Carroll's report of 20 April 1870 relating to the search for Jackson and the killing of Steven [Stephen] Cavendish [Caviness].
- National Archives and Records Administration (NARA). Washington, D.C. Lieutenant Bullis' report to Captain Carroll on the killing of Steven [Stephen] Cavendish [Caviness]. 19 April 1870.
- National Archives and Records Administration (NARA). Washington, D.C. Name Index to U.S. Military Academy

Cadet Application Papers, 1805-1866. Microfilm Serial M688. Microfilm Roll 1.
- National Archives and Records Administration (NARA). Washington, D.C. Returns from U.S. Military Posts 1800-1916. Microfilm Serial. M617. Microfilm Roll. 721.
- National Archives and Records Administration (NARA). General Order 95. Eighth Military District, 16 December 1851. RG 94.
- National Archives and Records Administration (NARA). General Order 11. Eighth Military District, 16 February 1852. RG 94.
- National Archives and Records Administration (NARA). Special Order 53. Department of Texas. 5 May 1856. RG 94. National Archives.
- National Park Services. Civil War Soldier & Sailor Archives.
- Records of the Fort McKavett Cemetery. Menard County, Texas. Compiled by Frederica Burt Wyatt. Submitted by Gloria B. Mayfield. Assisted by Coordinator, Dolores I. Bishop. 6 July 2000.
- Texas State Library & Archives Commission. Texas Ranger Frontier Battalion Service Records. Call Number 401-175.
- *The Army of the United States. Historical Sketches of Staff and Line With Portraits of General-in-Chief.* Edited by Theophilus Frances Rodenbrough. Bvt. Brigadier General and William L. Haskin. Major, First Artillery. 1896. Maynard, Merril & Co.
- Unites States Census. Census Years 1850, 1860, 1870, 1880, 1900.

INDEX

A
Abilene 83-85
Alamo 21, 94, 95, 145
Anderson, Ben 47
Apache (Indians) 1, 7, 15, 17, 37, 39, 65, 91-93, 99, 128, 138
Arkansas and Texas Land Company 21
Armstrong, Robert 95
Austin Mail Stage Line 145
Austin, Stephen F. 21, 26, 94,

B
Baker, Cullen M. 80
Ballinger 83, 85,
Baltimore, Charles W. 132
Battle of Adam's Hill 35
Beales, John Charles 21-24, 155, 158
Bear Creek 49, 70, 71, 72, 77, 81, 107
Beaumont, Eugene B. (Colonel) 39
Beef Trail Crossing 142
Bickerstaff, Benjamin F. 79, 80
Binford, T.A. 133
Black, Joseph A. 73
Black, William L. 53, 55
Bluff Creek 72
Bolton, Herbert E. 92, 97, 154
Bowie, James 29, 90, 94, 95, 96
Bowie, Rezin 29, 90, 94, 95, 96
Boyce, Reuben 107, 140
Brite, Charles 73
Brown, Dan 69, 70, 74
Brownsville 131, 147
Brownsville Affair 131, 132
Buchanan, David 95
Buffalo Gap 83

Buffalo Soldiers 3, 40, 46, 52, 64, 70, 101, 104, 122-136, 157, 158,
Bullis, John L. 67, 68, 70, 71, 72, 162

C

C. Bain & Company Stagecoach Line 138, 142, 148
Caddo (Indians) 2, 7
Callan 86, 90, 116, 118, 119
Callen City Company 118
Callan, James Joseph 118, 119, 120
Camp Logan Riot 131-134
Carlisle School 130, 131
Caviness, Stephen 69, 70, 71-73, 75, 77, 120, 162
Coke, Richard 67
Colbert's Ferry 146
Colorado and Red River Land Company 22
Colorado River 18, 19, 21, 22, 24, 30
Coopwood, Bethel 148
Comanche Indians 1, 2, 7, 8, 12, 15, 17, 26, 29, 34, 37, 38, 39, 52, 65, 91, 119, 126, 128, 129, 154, 155, 158, 159
Concho River 18, 19, 30, 31, 41, 146
Congressional Medal of Honor 51, 52, 68, 74, 127, 128, 134, 135
Conrad, Frank Eben 43
Copperas Creek 71
Corpus Christi de la Isleta (Ysleta) 18
Coryell, James 95
Cotton Road 147
Crane, Peter 69, 70
Crockett, David 94

D

Daniels, Benjamin Franklin "Ben" 78-88, 155
Daniels, Rufus 132, 133
Davis, Edmund J. 67
Davis, Tom 84
Delaware Spring 146
DeWitt, Green 21, 22
Devil's River 29
Dooley, M.A. 25

Doubleday, Abner 128
Doyle, Mathew 95
Dublin, Dell 107, 140
Dublin, Dick 107, 139, 140
Dublin, Role 107, 140
Durham, Elizabeth 62, 63, 75

E-F
Eckhardt, Charlie F. 90-92
Exter, Richard 21
Farley, J. 97
Father Fray Alonso Giraldo de Terreros 8, 9, 17
Father Fray Joseph de Santiesteban 8
Father Fray Miguel de Molina 8
Ferguson, James E. 134
Ficklan, Benjamin 142
Ficklan, Slaughter 142
Fisher, Henry Francis (Fisher-Miller Land Grant) 23-25, 157
Flipper, Henry Ossian 124
Flores, Bernardo de Miranda y 91
Flores, Joseph Antonio 9
Ford, John S. "RIP" 30
Fort Belknap 33, 146
Fort Concho 39, 52, 66, 68, 75, 128, 129, 140, 142, 148, 156, 162
Fort Clark 46, 53
Fort McIntosh 53
Fort McKavett 3-5, 17-60, 63, 65, 68, 69, 70, 73, 75, 76, 78, 82, 86, 87, 88, 89, 98, 100, 101, 104-107, 119, 120, 126-129, 139, 142, 144, 151, 152, 156, 159, 161-163
Fort Phantom Hill 146
Fort Worth & Rio Grande Railroad Company 1, 4, 86,102-103,118
Fort Yuma 146, 147

G
Galvan Juán 91
Gamel, William S. "Uncle Bill" 72
Gillespie, Tom 48, 49, 139
Gillett, James Buchanan 49, 50, 107, 139, 156

Gordon, George A. (Colonel) 40
Grant, James 22
Grierson, Benjamin Henry (Colonel) 125, 126, 128
Gutiérrez, Joseph 9

H-I
Ham, Caiphas K. 94, 95
Harrison, Dick 48, 49
Harvey, George 69, 70
Hatch, Edward 128
Hays, John Coffee "Jack" 29
Henry, Boston 66, 74, 75
Henry, Vida (Sergeant) 133, 134
Hext 86, 90, 116, 117, 121
Hext, James Bruten 116, 117
Hext, Robert Joseph 116, 117
Hill, Tom 83
Hoffman, William (General) 125
Holland, Jim 84
Honey Creek 72, 92, 93, 97
Houston Riot 131, 132
Hueco Tanks 146
Hulen, John A. (General) 134
Hunter, Samuel A. 121
Hutcheson, Grote 125

J-K
Jackson, Cynthia Louis "Lucy" Matilda 80, 81, 87
Jackson, John Monroe "Humpy" 50, 62-80, 113, 120, 159, 162
Jáuregui, Jacinto de Barrios y 91
Johnson, Ben 47
Jones, John B. 81
Junction City (Junction) 43, 50, 70, 81, 139
Kickapoo Creek 19, 33, 36, 52, 127
Kickapoo Indians 37, 38, 52
Kinney County 22
Kiowa Indians 26, 39, 128
Kirby, Henry (Lieutenant) 47

L-M

"Lanky Jim" 64-67, 75, 113
Las Moras Creek 22, 23, 24, 29, 30, 158
Llano Estacado 129
Lost Bowie Mine 90-94
Love, Jimmy 47
Mackenzie, Ranald Slidell (Colonel) 40-43, 51, 52, 70-75, 113, 126, 158, 162
Maringo 86, 116
Marshall, Albert 69, 70, 73, 74
Martin, Dean 72
Matamoros 147, 148
Mattes, Joseph 133
Maverick County 82
Maverick, Samuel 30
May, Charles (Lieutenant) 33
McCarthy, Tim 49
McCarthy, Tom 130
McCarty, Private 48
McCaslin, Thomas 95
McDougal Creek 138
McGee, Sergeant 48, 49
McKavett – Town 5, 17-62, 75, 76, 78, 86, 89, 98, 142, 144, 151
McKavett, Henry (Captain) 31
Meinke, Edwin G. 132, 133
Menard (County) 1-6, 7, 9-14, 18, 25-27, 37, 44, 49, 62, 66, 67, 72, 73, 76, 78, 82, 86, 88, 97, 98, 100, 103, 105-107, 112, 116-121, 142, 143, 151, 157, 162
Menardville 1-4, 38, 56, 63-75, 86, 98-115, 118, 140, 141, 144
Mescalero Indians 39
Milam, Benjamin Rush 22
Miller, Burchard 24, 25, 157
Mission Santa Cruz de San Sabá 7-16, 29, 90, 92
Moody, Horace 132, 133
Moore, F.M. 81, 84
Mower, Joseph A. 128
Murray, Charles 69, 70, 74

N-O
Neighbors, Robert 30
New Arkansas and Texas Land Company 22

Noxville 142
Nuestra Señora de la Limpia Conceptión del Socorro 18

P-Q
Peg Leg (Pegleg) 138-142
Peg Leg Pocket 117
Palace Saloon 85
Patton, Ross 132
Parrilla, Diego Ortiz 12, 14, 17, 18, 92, 93
Parks, Henry 119
Parks, Nancy Dorsey 119
Pershing, John J. "Black Jack" 129
Pinder, Hiram 130
Pope's Camp 146
Potter, Mack 140
Pratt, Richard Henry (Captain) 130-132, 155
Presidio San Luis de las Amarillas 9-17, 29, 30, 92-96, 100

R
Raney, Ira 132, 133
Range Canning Company 53, 56
Red River 2, 7, 22, 30, 34, 52, 93, 128, 131, 146, 156
Reynolds, Joseph Jones (General) 43, 127
Richey-DeFreest Land Company 118
Riley Mountains 92
Rio Grande River 18, 19, 21-23, 26, 29, 30, 53, 128, 147, 148
Rio Grande and Texas Land Company 22, 23
Río San Clemente 18
Ripperdá, Barón de 93
Robbers Roost 139
Robertson, Peter 69, 112, 113
Robinson, Joshua D. 25
Royuela, José Manuel 21, 22

S
Saldaña, María Dolores Soto y 21
Saline 73, 86, 90, 116, 119-121
San Antonio-El Paso Stage Line (Southern Stage Line) 145, 147
San Antonio-San Diego Stage Line (Southern Stage Line) 139, 142

San Antonio de Senecú 18
San Carlos 30
San Pedro Creek 21
San Saba, Camp 3, 26, 29, 53
San Saba, Presidio (see Presidio San Luis de las Amarillas)
San Saba River 1, 2, 4, 14, 17, 19, 30, 37, 54, 63, 92, 93, 96, 100, 107, 112, 138, 139, 143
San Saba Valley 1, 17, 34, 65
Scabtown 26, 43, 44, 47, 53, 60
Shafter, William Rufus 40, 41, 52, 128
Sherman, William Tecumseh 51
Smart, Cynthia Ann 62
Smith, Edmund Kirby 36
Smith, Persifor (General) 31
Smith, Tullius B. "Tully" 112-114
Smith, William F. 30
Snow, Keenland S. (Major) 132
South Llano River 19, 139
Splittgerber Stage Stand 142, 143
Staked Plains Horror 129
Stance, Emanuel 40, 51, 52, 127, 128
Stevenson, George 47, 48
Stowers, Freddie 135
Streeter, Samuel T. 72, 73

T-U-V
Terán, Felip de Rabago y 17
Texas Rangers 26, 34, 49, 50, 82, 105, 107, 139, 150
Texas United States Mail Line 145
Thorino, Luis 10
Trans-Pecos 30
de Urrutia, Don Toribio 12, 13
US Military Units
   1st Texas Mounted Rifles 36
   2nd Dragoons 33, 152
   4th Cavalry 39, 40, 46,
   4th Infantry 66
   8th Infantry 29, 31-35, 40, 152
   9th Cavalry 40, 51, 64, 66, 68, 69, 124-128, 135
   10th Cavalry 46, 47, 52, 122, 124-130, 135

22nd Infantry 46
24 Infantry 40, 41, 52, 124, 126, 134, 135
25th Infantry 122, 124, 127, 135
38th Infantry 40, 41
41st Infantry 40, 41, 52, 122, 124, 126
Vaden John Wesley 78-89, 155
Vásquez, Joseph 10
Vehlein, Joseph 22
Viejo Creek (See Bear Creek) 49, 70-72, 77, 81, 107

W-X-Y-Z
Wagoner, George Henry 117
Wagoner Ville 117
Wallace, Jesse 78
Watkins, William 130
Western Cattle Trail 141
West Point Military Academy 31, 40, 124
Whiting, William H.C. 29, 30, 138, 159, 160
Wichita (Indians) 2, 7, 8
Wilks, Jacob W. 51
Wilson, Stephen Julian 21
Woodbury, John Lucius 22

About The Author

Cliff Caldwell has continually cultivated his interest in western history since boyhood. After a stint in United States Marine Corps during the Vietnam War, and a successful thirty-five-year career working for several Fortune 500 corporations, Cliff is now retired and free to pursue his interests as a historian and writer on a full-time basis. Cliff holds a Bachelor of Science degree in business and is the author of several books and published works, including *Dead Right, The Lincoln County War, Guns of the Lincoln County War, A Day's Ride From Here Volumes I and II, John Simpson Chisum, The Cattle King of the Pecos Revisited,* and *Texas Lawmen 1835-1899, The Good and the Bad, Texas Lawmen 1900-1940, More of the Good and the Bad,* and his latest work – *Robert Kelsey Wylie, Forgotten Cattle King of Texas.*

Cliff is recognized as an accomplished historian and researcher on the American West. He is a member of Western Writers of America, Inc., the Wild West History Association, Texas State Historical Association and the Buffalo Bill Historical Center. When not deeply involved in writing, Cliff volunteers some of his time doing research for the Peace Officers Memorial Foundation of Texas.

Cliff and his wife live in the Hill Country of Texas, near Mountain Home.

www.ingramcontent.com/pod-product-compliance
Lightning Source LLC
Chambersburg PA
CBHW020948230426
43666CB00005B/230